The Cabinet Minister

The Cabinet Minister

A farce in four acts

by
Sir Arthur Wing Pinero

Oberon Books
Birmingham · England

This edition published in 1987 by Oberon Books Limited
Mill Street, Aston, Birmingham B6 4BS, England. Telephone 021-359 2088.

James Hogan   *Publishing Director*
Andrew Purcell CA   *Managing Director*
Robert Weaver MIOP   *Production Director*

First published by William Heinemann, London, 1892.

Produced and printed in England by Kynoch Dataset Limited, Birmingham.
Cover painting by Michael Garady.
Text typeset in 'Garamond'.

ISBN 1 870259 08 4

Introduction

The Cabinet Minister is not overtly a play of ideas but we are left in no doubt about Pinero's view of a divided Victorian Society. This skilfully constructed, unashamedly theatrical work, cannot fail to entertain and even stimulate a sophisticated modern audience, consisting of people who must be far removed in type and temperament from well-to-do Victorian theatregoers. The well-bred rich find themselves under siege against low-bred upstarts and are wickedly satirised in a way that must still delight audiences a hundred years on.

Sir Arthur Wing Pinero's farces have always been admired for their sure fire theatrical effect, though his dramas, with one or two notable exceptions, have fared less well. Pinero's plays are judged to be short on intellectual substance, though he was far too clever a dramatist to rely on empty comic situations beloved of the light comedy hacks of the late Victorian era. His preoccupation with detail and his keen interest in ensuring that his plays were accurately interpreted according to his intentions indicates that he was a committed dramatist by nature and had, to his own way of thinking, something to say.

In his own lifetime, however, Pinero was described as a craftsman who had little sympathy with modern ideas. After all, his contemporaries included Ibsen and Zola who led the avante garde movement at the time. So it was safe to dismiss Pinero as a minor playwright in terms of content, while recognising him as a craftsman in terms of execution. But his best plays have survived for over one hundred years because they do contain substance — a deep respect for human nature.

The durability of *The Cabinet Minister* rests largely on the sharply observed characters. We find ourselves in the presence of a group of establishment figures who are mixing with mildly subversive hangers-on. Pinero was not a polemical playwright, but *The Cabinet Minister* involves characters who either challenge or caricature the social excesses of the day.

First performed in 1890, *The Cabinet Minister* is a good, solid commercial piece — a hybrid of farce/comedy — in which the characters are conceived as distinct establishment, and anti-establishment types. Sir Julian Twombley, the cabinet minister of the title is a world-weary politician to whom opening a new street is a bore. Because Pinero is such a meticulous craftsman, it is unlikely that his sketch of a minister of the crown, who never reads a newspaper in case it causes him undue worry, is meant to be anything other than satirical. His wife, Lady Twombley, is an extravagant Society hostess whose obsession with social prestige, and a spectacular wardrobe, pushes her into serious debt. The siblings of this marriage, Brooke and Imogen are spoiled, over privileged stereotypes whose lifestyle comes under attack from their rebel cousin, Valentine White.

Valentine, in turn, declares that he left England to get away from all the 'sham' and 'ceremony' and find freedom. He also voices disappointment in Imogen who has, to his way of thinking, lost her innocence to become a social butterfly.

How neatly Pinero turns Valentine's judgement on its head by demonstrating that Valentine's free thinking is also determined by a limited set of values. It may, however, be reading too much significance into Pinero's intentions to suggest that Valentine's journey to South Africa, and quick departure to other shores, was intended to be a political comment. Nevertheless, one must give credit to for his topicality in placing his characters in such an apt social and political environment.

Having created such entertaining and credible characters, Pinero introduces into the turmoil of debt, disaster and difficulty (his own alliteration) Mr Joseph Lebanon a money-lender described as a 'common semitic type'. Lebanon is an anti-hero if ever there was one. His parasitic grasp on the plight of the frivolous Twombley family proves to be a chastening experience for everyone involved. This is not the place to reveal the outcome of the story but Pinero's happy ending, rather too pat to be true, does aim at a blow at Society's aspirations to wealth and position. Lebanon is the perfect foil who demonstrates to the others that money can be a classless commodity. For as we witness the financial salvation of the Twombleys, we cannot be but conscious of the despair that might have followed if one of them had not resorted to a little 'forgiveable' cheating.

Pinero's theatrical career spanned neary sixty years from 1874 to 1932. He was an actor before becoming a dramatist which, no doubt, explains why his characters are so actable. His reputation still rests, however, on a handful of farces including *The Magistrate* and *Dandy Dick*, plus two other important works, *The Second Mrs Tanqueray* and *Trelawny of the Wells*, all written between 1885 and 1898. *The Cabinet Minister* ranks as one of Pinero's best farces of this productive period, though it is not always recognised as a play in which rigid social convention, class division and discrimination are mischievously exposed to the naked eye of an audience which, no doubt, consisted of the very types portrayed in the play itself.

In *The Cabinet Minister* Pinero's mastery of stagecraft is certainly apparent in line after line. Exposition, plot, sub-plot, characterisation and denouement coalesce successfully into a typically fast-moving farce which can hardly fail to satisfy. The situations which Pinero creates for his principal characters are sustained through all four acts and tidily resolved at the end, even if the allusions to Society's greed, envy, ambition, and wealth, are overtaken by theatrical effects. The play appeals to the heart rather than the mind, but Pinero's feeling for human nature and his grasp of Victorian values explain why his comedies have survived well when those of his contemporaries, with the obvious exception of Oscar Wilde, have not.

James Hogan
DECEMBER 1987

ROYAL COURT THEATRE.

UNDER THE MANAGEMENT OF MRS. JOHN WOOD.

ON WEDNESDAY, APRIL 23rd,

At 8 o'clock,

WILL BE ACTED FOR THE FIRST TIME

AN ORIGINAL FARCE IN FOUR ACTS, CALLED

THE CABINET MINISTER,

BY

A. W. PINERO.

EARL OF DRUMDURRIS (in the GUARDS)	Mr. RICHARD SAUNDERS.
VISCOUNT ABERBROTHOCK (his Son)	• • • •
RIGHT HON. SIR JULIAN TWOMBLEY, G.C.M.G., M.P. (Secretary of State for the —— Department) . .	Mr. ARTHUR CECIL.
BROOKE TWOMBLEY (his Son)	Mr. E. ALLAN AYNESWORTH.
MACPHAIL OF BALLOCHEEVIN	Mr. BRANDON THOMAS.
MR. JOSEPH LEBANON . .	Mr. WEEDON GROSSMITH.
VALENTINE WHITE (Lady Twombley's Nephew) . .	Mr. HERBERT WARING.
MR. MITFORD * (Sir Julian's Private Secretary). . .	Mr. FRANK FARREN.
THE MUNKITTRICK . .	Mr. JOHN CLULOW.
PROBYN (A Servant) . .	Mr. ERNEST PATON.

DOWAGER COUNTESS OF DRUMDURRIS . . .	Miss R. G. LE THIÈRE.
LADY EUPHEMIA VIBART (her Daughter)	Miss ISABEL ELLISSEN.
COUNTESS OF DRUMDURRIS .	Miss EVA MOORE.
LADY TWOMBLEY . . .	Mrs. JOHN WOOD.
IMOGEN (her Daughter) . .	Miss FLORENCE TANNER.
LADY MACPHAIL . . .	Mrs. EDMUND PHELPS.
HON. MRS. GAYLUSTRE (a Young Widow trading as Mauricette et Cie., 17A, Plunkett Street, Mayfair) . .	Miss ROSINA FILIPPI.
ANGÈLE	Miss MARIANNE CALDWELL
MISS MUNKITTRICK . .	Miss FLORENCE HARRINGTON.

THE SCENERY IS DESIGNED AND PAINTED BY T. W. HALL.

---

* *Subsequently changed to* MELTON.

Act One
DEBT
At Sir Julian Twombley's, Chesterfield Gardens. May.

Act Two
DIFFICULTIES
At Sir Julian's again. July.

Act Three
DISASTER
At Drumdurris Castle, Perthshire. August.

Act Four
DANCING
The same place. The next day.

Characters

Right Hon. Sir Julian Twombley, G.C.M.G., M.P., *Secretary of State for the * * * Department*
Lady Twombley
Brooke Twombley, *their son*
Imogen, *their daughter*
Dowager Countess of Drumdurris
Lady Euphemia Vibart, *her daughter*
Earl of Drumdurris, *in the Guards*
Countess of Drumdurris
Viscount Aberbrothock, *their baby son*
Lady Macphail
Macphail of Ballocheevin, *her son*
Valentine White, *Lady Twombley's nephew*
Hon. Mrs. Gaylustre, *a young widow trading as Mauricette et Cie., 17a Plunkett Street, Mayfair*
Mr. Joseph Lebanon
Mr. Melton, *Sir Julian's Private Secretary*
The Munkittrick
Miss Munkittrick
Probyn, *a servant*
Angèle, *a maid*

The First Act

Debt

[*The scene is a conservatory built and decorated in Moorish style, in the house of the Rt. Hon.* SIR JULIAN TWOMBLEY, *MP., Chesterfield Gardens, London. A fountain is playing, and tall palms lend their simple elegance to the elaborate Algerian magnificence of the place. The drawing-rooms are just beyond the curtained entrances. It is a May afternoon*]

[BROOKE TWOMBLEY, *a good-looking but insipid young man of about two-and-twenty, faultlessly dressed for the afternoon, enters, and sits dejectedly, turning over some papers*]

Brooke Twombley I've done it. Such an afternoon's work – what! [*Reading*] "Schedule of the Debts of Mr Brooke Twombley. [*Turning over sheet after sheet*] Tradesmen. Betting transactions. Baccarat. Miscellaneous amusements. Sundries. Extras."

[PROBYN, *a servant in powder and livery, is crossing the conservatory, when he sees* BROOKE]

Probyn Oh, Mr Brooke.

Brooke Twombley [*Slipping the schedule into his pocket*] Eh!

Probyn I didn't know you were in, sir. Her ladyship told me to give you this, Mr Brooke – quietly.

[*He hands* BROOKE *a letter which he has taken from his pocket*]

Brooke Twombley [*Glancing at the envelope*] The Mater. Thank you. [*A little cough is heard. He looks toward the drawing-room*] Is anyone there?

Probyn Mrs Gaylustre, sir.

Brooke Twombley The dressmaker! What does she want?

Probyn She told Phipps, Miss Imogen's maid, sir, that she was anxious to see the effect of her ladyship's and Miss Imogen's gowns when they get back from the Drawing-Room.

Brooke Twombley You should take her upstairs.

Probyn	Beg your pardon, Mr Brooke, but we've always understood that when Mrs Gaylustre calls in the morning she's a dressmaker, and when she calls in the afternoon she's a lady.
Brooke Twombley	Oh, very well; it's awfully confusing. [PROBYN *goes out.* BROOKE *reads the letter*] "My sweet child. For heaven's sake let me have your skeddle, or whatever you call your list of debts, directly. I'll do my best to get you out of your scrape, though <u>how</u> I can't think. I'm desperately short of money, and altogether – as my poor dear father used to say – things are as blue as old Stilton. If your pa finds out what a muddle I'm in, I fear he'll throw up public life and bury us in the country, and then good-bye to my dear boy's and girl's prospects. So if I contrive to clear you once more, don't do it again, my poppet, or you'll break the heart of your loving mother, Kitty Twombley." The Mater's a brick – what! But I wonder if she has any notion how much it tots up to.

[*He places the letter upon the back of a large saddle-bag arm-chair while he takes out the schedule*]

Three thousand seven hundred and fifty-six, nought, two. What!

[PROBYN *enters*]

Probyn	A young man wants to see you, Mr Brooke.
Brooke Twombley	Who is it?
Probyn	No card, sir – and rather queerly dressed. Says he has a wish to shake hands with you on the doorstep.
Brooke Twombley	Oh, I say! He mustn't, you know – what!
Probyn	I don't quite like the look of him, sir; gives the name of White – Mr Valentine White.
Brooke Twombley	Why, that's my cousin!
Probyn	Cousin, sir! I beg pardon.
Brooke Twombley	Where is he?

[BROOKE *goes out quickly, followed by* PROBYN. *The* HON. MRS GAYLUSTRE, *an attractive, self-possessed, mischievous-looking woman, of not more than thirty, very fashionably dressed, enters from the drawing-room*]

Mrs Gaylustre   How very charming! Lady Twombley's latest fad, the
Algerian conservatory. And there was a time when
a sprig of geranium on the window-sill would have
contented her. [*Looking at a photograph of* LADY TWOMBLEY
upon the table] There she is – Kitty Twombley. In one
of my gowns too. Kitty Twombley, once Kitty White,
the daughter of a poor farmer down in Cleverton. Ah,
when young Mr Julian Twombley came canvassing
Farmer White's vote he found you innocently scrubbing
the bricks, I suppose! And now! [*With a courtesy*] Lady
Twombley, wife of a Cabinet Minister and Patroness
Extraordinary of that deserving young widow, Fanny
Gaylustre! [*She sits surveying the portraits upon the table*]
Ha, ha! I'll turn you all to account some fine day. Why
shouldn't I finish as well as the dairy-fed daughter of
a Devonshire yokel? What on earth is wrong with my
bonnet? [*She puts her hand up behind her head and finds*
LADY TWOMBLEY'*s letter which* BROOKE *had left on the back of
the chair*] Lady Twombley's writing. [*Reading*] "My sweet
child. For heaven's sake let me have your skeddle – " [*She
sits up suddenly and devours the contents of the letter*] Oh!
[*Reading aloud*] "I'm desperately short of money! Things
are as blue as old Stilton! If your pa finds out – !" My
word!

Brooke Twombley   [*Heard speaking outside*] My dear Valentine, why shouldn't
you come in – what?

[MRS GAYLUSTRE *creeps round in front of the table and
disappears with the letter in her hand as* BROOKE *enters,
dragging in* VALENTINE WHITE, *a roughly-dressed, handsome
young fellow of about six-and-twenty, bronzed and bearded*]

Valentine White   Now, Brooke, you know I cut away from England years
ago because I couldn't endure ceremony of any kind.

Brooke Twombley   I'm not treating you with ceremony – what!

Valentine White   [*Looking about him*] Phew! The atmosphere's charged
with it. That fellow with his hair powdered nearly sent
me running down the street like a mad dog.

Brooke Twombley   Where the deuce have you been for the last six or eight
years?

Valentine White   Where? Oh, buy a geography; call it, "Explorations of
Valentine White in Search of Freedom," and there you
have it.

Brooke Twombley	Freedom!
Valentine White	Blessed freedom from forms, shams, and ceremonies of all sorts and descriptions.
Brooke Twombley	Why, you left us for South Africa. Didn't South Africa satisfy you?
Valentine White	Satisfy me! I joined the expedition to Bangwaketsi. What were the consequences?
Brooke Twombley	Fever?
Valentine White	Worse. There's no ceremony about fever. No, Brooke, I was snubbed by a major in the Kalahari Desert, because I didn't dress for dinner.
Brooke Twombley	Then we heard of you herding filthy cattle in Mexico.
Valentine White	Yes, at Durango. I enjoyed that, till some younger sons of the nobility came out and left cards at my hut. I afterwards drove a railway engine in Bolivia.
Brooke Twombley	By Jove, how awful – what! Wasn't that sufficiently beastly rough?
Valentine White	My dear fellow, would you believe it – I got hold of a stoker who was a decayed British baronet! The affected way in which that man shovelled on coals was unendurable. So I've come back, hopelessly wise.
Brooke Twombley	Serve you right for kicking at refinement and good form and all that sort of thing. What!
Valentine White	[*Mimicking* BROOKE] Varnish, and veneer, and all that sort of thing – what!
Brooke Twombley	Oh, confound you! Well, you'll dine here at a quarter to eight, Val, won't you?
Valentine White	Dine in Chesterfield Gardens! Thirteen courses and eight wines! Heaven forgive you, Brooke.
Brooke Twombley	Look here, you shall eat on the floor with a wooden spoon.
Valentine White	Thank you – even your floors are too highly polished. Tell Aunt Kitty and little Imogen that I shall walk in Kensington Gardens tomorrow morning at ten.
Brooke Twombley	Little Imogen! Haw, haw!
Valentine White	Well?

Brooke Twombley	I think it will pretty considerably wound your susceptibilities to hear that my sister Imogen is being presented by the Mater this afternoon.
Valentine White	[*In horror*] Presented!
Brooke Twombley	Presented at Court – Drawing Room, you know.
Valentine White	How dare they! Poor little child!
Brooke Twombley	Haw, haw! If you'll wait a few minutes you'll see an imposing display of trains and feathers. Some of them are coming on here after the ceremony to drink tea, I believe.
Valentine White	Trains and feathers! Good gracious, Brooke, Imogen must have grown up!
Brooke Twombley	Here's her portrait – what!
Valentine White	[*Staring at the portrait*] I am right, Brooke – she <u>has</u> grown up!
Brooke Twombley	Haw!
Valentine White	Eight years ago she was a romp, with a frock that always had a tear in it, and a head like a cornfield in the wind. Just look at this! While I've been away they've given her a new frock and brushed her hair. What an awful change!
	[PROBYN *appears at the conservatory entrance*]
Probyn	Lady Euphemia Vibart.
	[LADY EUPHEMIA VIBART, *a handsome, distinguished-looking, and elegantly dressed girl of about twenty, enters. She scarcely notices* VALENTINE *who bows formally*]
Lady Euphemia Vibart	No-one has returned yet, Brooke?
Brooke Twombley	Effie, don't you recollect Mr White?
Lady Euphemia Vibart	Oh! How do you do? [*She shakes hands with him in an affected manner*] We are distantly related, I remember.
Valentine White	Lady Euphemia, I join you in remembering the relationship – and the distance.
Lady Euphemia Vibart	Oh, I didn't mean that, Mr White. At any rate, we were excellent friends many years ago when our cousin Imogen used to give us tea in her schoolroom. She will be <u>too</u> rejoiced at your return.
Brooke Twombley	[*At the window*] Hullo, I think pa has come home.

Valentine White	Good-bye Lady Euphemia.
Brooke Twombley	I say, Effie, Mr White won't stay.
Lady Euphemia Vibart	[*Indifferently*] What a pity!
Brooke Twombley	He has turned against civilisation, you know, and has become a sort of pleasant cannibal.
Lady Euphemia Vibart	A cannibal! That is too interesting. Pray remain, Mr White. My brother, Lord Drumdurris, is on duty at the Palace today and is coming on here. We all knew each other as children. He will be too delighted.
Valentine White	I recollect Lord Vibart, as he then was, very well. He once burnt me with a red hot poker.
Lady Euphemia Vibart	Good humouredly, I am sure. Perhaps you have not heard that he married Lady Egidia Cardelloe, Lord Struddock's second daughter, about two years ago. If you stay you will meet her also.
Valentine White	Ah, I am afraid I – I –
Lady Euphemia Vibart	You will find her too enchanting.
Brooke Twombley	No, he won't. She's not tattooed or anything.
Lady Euphemia Vibart	They have a little son, just five months old, who is too divine.
Brooke Twombley	Ah, now, if you boiled the baby it might be to Val's taste.
Lady Euphemia Vibart	As they have been constantly travelling, Egidia is only just presented today by my mother. You recollect Lady Drumdurris, my mother?
Valentine White	Perfectly.
Brooke Twombley	[*Poking* VALENTINE *in the side*] Old Lady Drum!
Lady Euphemia Vibart	My mother will be too charmed to meet you again.
	[PROBYN *enters*]
Probyn	[*To* BROOKE] Sir Julian is coming into the conservatory, sir.
Brooke Twombley	Pa!
	[PROBYN *goes out*]
Lady Euphemia Vibart	Oh, dear Sir Julian!
	[*She runs out*]
Valentine White	Look sharp, Brooke. Let me out.

Brooke Twombley	Val, I'll tell you what. Come upstairs and smoke a cigarette in my room, and I'll bring the Mater and Imogen to you on the quiet when the people are gone.
Valentine White	Why, Brooke, do you think that Aunt Kitty and Imogen want a roving relative on the premises who isn't worth tuppence!
Brooke Twombley	Bosh! Look out, here's pa! He seems awfully mumpish. Come on.

[*He takes* VALENTINE *out. Directly they are gone* LADY EUPHEMIA *re-enters with* SIR JULIAN TWOMBLEY, *an aristocratic but rather weak-looking man of about fifty-five, wearing his Ministerial uniform*]

Lady Euphemia Vibart	Are you pleased to get back, uncle?
Sir Julian Twombley	[*Emphatically*] Yes.

[LADY EUPHEMIA *places him in the arm-chair. He sinks into it with a sigh*]

Lady Euphemia Vibart	How is your neuralgia?
Sir Julian Twombley	Intense. It has been so ever since –
Lady Euphemia Vibart	[*Putting her smelling-bottle to his nose*] Ever since?
Sir Julian Twombley	Ever since I took Office. Thank you.
Lady Euphemia Vibart	Was it a very brilliant Drawing-Room?
Sir Julian Twombley	I think it must have been. I have been more than usually trodden upon.
Lady Euphemia Vibart	Did you catch a glimpse of Aunt Kitty or of any of our people?
Sir Julian Twombley	I <u>heard</u> Lady Twombley. What inexhaustible spirit she has! Euphemia, my dear, I confide in you. But for Lady Twombley I could never endure the badgering, the browbeating, the hackling, for which I seem especially selected.
Lady Euphemia Vibart	It's <u>too</u> unjust.
Sir Julian Twombley	Oh, I know I am going to have a bad time in the House tonight!
Lady Euphemia Vibart	Don't dwell upon it, uncle.
Sir Julian Twombley	Euphemia!

[He jumps up almost fiercely]

Lady Euphemia Vibart Uncle Julian!

Sir Julian Twombley Certain members of the Opposition are going too far. They regard me as a bull in the arena. They goad me, they pierce me with questions. And then, the lack of journalistic sympathy! Look here!

[He stealthily produces a newspaper from his pocket]

Lady Euphemia Vibart *[Reproachfully]* Uncle Julian, you've bought a newspaper. You promised aunt you never would.

Sir Julian Twombley H'm! I would have you know, Euphemia, that I have not absolutely broken my pledge to Lady Twombley. I made Harris, the coachman, purchase this. As you drive home drop it out of your carriage window.

[As LADY EUPHEMIA *takes the paper from him her eyes fall upon a paragraph]*

Lady Euphemia Vibart Oh! Do they mean you, uncle?

Sir Julian Twombley Without doubt.

Lady Euphemia Vibart *[Reading]* "The square peg!"

Sir Julian Twombley Hush! The servant!

*[*LADY EUPHEMIA *crams the paper into her pocket.* PROBYN *enters, carrying a small music-easel with some music on it and a flute in a case]*

Probyn Here, Sir Julian?

Lady Euphemia Vibart Oh, do play, uncle!

Sir Julian Twombley *[To* PROBYN*]* Thank you.

Lady Euphemia Vibart It will soothe you.

Sir Julian Twombley *[Taking the flute from* PROBYN*]* My only vice, Euphemia.

*[*PROBYN *goes out.* SIR JULIAN *sounds a mournful note]*

This little friend has inspired some of my most conspicuous oratorical triumphs. It has furnished me with many a cutting rejoinder for question time. *[He sounds another note]* Ah, I know I am going to have such a bad night in the House.

[He plays. MRS GAYLUSTRE *enters with* BROOKE*]*

Lady Euphemia Vibart *[To herself]* That woman!

Mrs Gaylustre	[*To* LADY EUPHEMIA] How do you do?
	[LADY EUPHEMIA *stares, inclines her head slightly, and goes back to* BROOKE]
	[*To herself*] Haughty wretch!
Sir Julian Twombley	Mrs Gaylustre!
Mrs Gaylustre	Oh, Sir Julian, don't, don't stop!
Sir Julian Twombley	I thought I was alone with Lady Euphemia.
Mrs Gaylustre	I am waiting to see dear Lady Twombley. Oh, do permit me to hear that sweet instrument!
Sir Julian Twombley	Pray sit down!
	[SIR JULIAN *resumes his seat and plays a plaintive melody.* MRS GAYLUSTRE *listens in a rapt attitude*]
Lady Euphemia Vibart	[*To* BROOKE] That person is too odious to me.
Brooke Twombley	Several people have taken her up.
Lady Euphemia Vibart	Somehow, being taken up is what she suggests.
Brooke Twombley	She seems a sort of society mermaid – half a lady and half a milliner – what! Only it bothers you to know where the one leaves off and the other begins. Who is she?
Lady Euphemia Vibart	In prehistoric days she was a Miss Lebanon. Lord Bulpitt's son, Percy Gaylustre, met her at Nice – or somewhere.
Brooke Twombley	Oh, yes, and he married her – or something.
Lady Euphemia Vibart	Yes, and now she's a widow – or something.
Brooke Twombley	Why does the Mater encourage her?
Lady Euphemia Vibart	Because Aunt Kate is too good-hearted and impressionable. But, as a rule, I think Mrs Gaylustre makes a considerable reduction to those who ask her to their parties. [MRS GAYLUSTRE *is bending over* SIR JULIAN *and turning his music*] Look!
	[PROBYN *appears at the entrance*]
Probyn	Here's Sir Julian, my lady.
Brooke Twombley	Hullo, Mater!
	[LADY TWOMBLEY, *a handsome, bright, good-humoured woman, dressed magnificently in Court dress, enters.* PROBYN *retires, and* SIR JULIAN *stops playing*]

Lady Twombley	[*Kissing* BROOKE] Well, Brooke, darling, have you wanted your mother? [*Kissing* LADY EUPHEMIA] Effie, how sweet you look! What a dream of a bonnet! [*Nods to* MRS GAYLUSTRE] How d'ye do, Mrs Gaylustre? Why, pa! [*She bends over him and kisses him*] You're worried – you've been playing your whistle.
Sir Julian Twombley	Flute, Katherine.
Lady Twombley	I mean flute. It was my brother Bob who always played a whistle when the crops were poor or the lambs fell sickly.
Sir Julian Twombley	I had not the advantage of your brother Robert's acquaintance.
Lady Twombley	Where's Imogen? Imogen!
Imogen	[*Outside*] Mamma!
Lady Twombley	Come and show yourself to pa.
	[IMOGEN *enters in her Court dress, a pretty girl of about eighteen*]
Imogen	Effie, dear! Well, Brooke!
Lady Twombley	[*To* SIR JULIAN] Look at her!
Sir Julian Twombley	Quite charming!
Imogen	Well, papa, have you nothing to say to me?
Sir Julian Twombley	My dear, I hesitate to address such a magnificent creature.
Imogen	[*Bowing to* SIR JULIAN] Mamma, I think that gentleman wishes to be presented to me. I have no objection, if you consider him a person I ought to know.
Lady Twombley	[*Kissing* IMOGEN] Ah, Julian, our sweet child!
Sir Julian Twombley	[*Taking* IMOGEN's *hand*] My dear.
Imogen	[*With dignity*] I am pleased to make your acquaintance. I've heard you mentioned very kindly by my little friend, Imogen Twombley. Pray sit down, and I'll sit on your lap. [*She sits on* SIR JULIAN's *knee and puts her arm round his neck*] Oh, papa, I have been so nervous!
Mrs Gaylustre	I quite sympathise. I was shockingly nervous when I was presented.
Imogen	[*Rising hastily*] Mrs Gaylustre – I didn't see you.

Lady Twombley	[*To* BROOKE *and* LADY EUPHEMIA] Dear old Lady Leeke, whose wheels we locked in the Park, said she had heard Imogen's name mentioned fifty times. Mrs Charlie Lessingham declares nothing prettier has been seen since her own first season. And it's true — that's the best of it! I saw the child make her courtesy; I was determined I would. I entered the Throne Room just before her and tumbled through anyhow, with one eye straight in front of me and the other screwed round towards my girl. There was a general shudder — it was at my squint.
Sir Julian Twombley	I trust not, Katherine.
Lady Twombley	When I did get through they gave me my train as much as to say: "If this belongs to you, take it home as soon as possible." But there I stuck in the doorway, not budging an inch. I didn't care how the officials whispered, and waved, and beckoned; I stood my ground. And then, Julian, then my breath nearly went from me, for I saw her coming! Effie, it was lovely! Brooke, you would have been proud of your sister! Her cheeks were like the outside leaf of a Duchesse de Vallombrosa rose, and her eyes like two dewdrops on the top of it; and she had just enough fright in her little heart to make her feathers tremble. Then she courtesied. Ah, if she had stumbled I should have been by her side in an instant — who would have blamed me? I'm her mother! — but she didn't. No, she floated towards me — dipping, and dipping, and dipping, again and again, as smoothly and gracefully as a swan swimming backward!

[LADY TWOMBLEY *embraces* IMOGEN]

Lady Euphemia Vibart	I am <u>too</u> glad, Aunt Kitty.
Brooke Twombley	Awfully satisfactory — what!
Sir Julian Twombley	I remember Lady Liphook's daughter Miriam falling and rolling over in the season of '85.
Lady Twombley	Lor' how sorry I feel for anybody who isn't a mother! But, I say, there's a bit that wants taking in there. [*Pinching up the shoulder of* IMOGEN's *dress*] Gaylustre, you must tell your woman, Antoinette, this won't do.
Mrs Gaylustre	Oh, Lady Twombley — please!

[MRS GAYLUSTRE *puts her handkerchief to her eyes*]

Lady Twombley	My dear, pray forgive me! I really forgot where we were.

Mrs Gaylustre	[*To* LADY TWOMBLEY *with a little sob*] You wouldn't hurt my feelings wilfully, I know.
Lady Twombley	Not for the world. But it's a little confusing, mixing up business with pleasure. Imogen, let Lady Effie and Mrs Gaylustre hear you play your lovely harp, but don't let the nasty thing hurt your fingers. Brooke, I want to speak to you.

[LADY EUPHEMIA *and* IMOGEN *stroll out, followed by* MRS GAYLUSTRE]

Sir Julian Twombley	[*Mournfully*] I'll dress now, Katherine, and go down.
Lady Twombley	Lor', pa, don't speak as if you were thinking of our tomb at Kensal Geen.
Sir Julian Twombley	Competent authorities assure me there is quiet to be found in the tomb; I anticipate nothing of that kind where I am going tonight.

[*He goes out.* LADY TWOMBLEY *watches his going, then turns to* BROOKE *sharply*]

Lady Twombley	Well, have you got it?
Brooke Twombley	My – er –
Lady Twombley	Your skeddle.

[BROOKE *hands his schedule to* LADY TWOMBLEY]

Lady Twombley	There's a dear boy. [*She turns over the leaves, gradually her face assumes a look of horror*] "Total, three thousand – !"

[*She folds the schedule, puts it in her pocket, and faces* BROOKE *fiercely with her hands clenched*]

You imp!

[*She boxes his right ear soundly*]

Brooke Twombley	Mater!
Lady Twombley	You villain!

[*She boxes his left ear*]

Brooke Twombley	Don't Mater!
Lady Twombley	Three thousand pounds! Three thousand times I wish you had never been born! I – I – [*She breaks down, puts her arms round* BROOKE*'s neck, and cries*] Oh, Brooke, my dear, forgive your poor mother's vile temper. I've made my Brooke's head ache. Oh, my gracious!

Brooke Twombley	Don't fret, Mater. If you're run rather low at Scott's –
Lady Twombley	Scott's, Brooke! When I creep into that bank now and ask for my pass-book I have to hold on to the edge of the counter, I feel so sick and giddy.
Brooke Twombley	Oh, very well then, Mater, I can wait. Mr Nazareth, of Burlington Street, will accommodate me for a time; a couple of bills, you know, at three and six months – what?
Lady Twombley	[*Speaking in a whisper*] Brooky, Brooky, I've thought of those dreadful things for myself.
Brooke Twombley	For yourself, Mater! Why, you can always get the right side of pa.
Lady Twombley	Brooke! Brooky, I must tell you. Just now poor pa has no right side.
Brooke Twombley	Mater!
Lady Twombley	It's as much as the dear man can do to get a rattle out of his keys. For a long time, Brooke, we've all been outrunning the constable.
Brooke Twombley	Really, Mater, I ought to have been consulted before.
Lady Twombley	I know, Brooke, but I couldn't face my boy's reproaches.
Brooke Twombley	Pa must have been inexcusably reckless – what?
Lady Twombley	No, it's my fault, every bit of it. [*A pretty melody on the harp is heard*] Brooke, never marry a country-bred girl as your pa did. When he fell in love with me I was content with three frocks a year – think of that! – and had to twist up my own hats. And I could have done it for ever down at Cleverton, but I didn't stand the transplanting. Oh, I'll never forget how the fine folks snubbed me and sneered at me when I came to town. Brooke, my son, I declare to goodness that for ten long years I never saw a nose that wasn't turned up! And then pa got his baronetcy, and old Lady Drumdurris gave us her forefinger to shake, and that was it. But it was too late; I was spoilt by that time. I had been too long fishing for friends with dances, and dinners, and drags, and race-parties, and all sorts of bait; and when the time came for a few people to like me for my own stupid, rough self I'd got into the way of scattering sovereigns as freely as I used to sprinkle mignonette seed in my little garden at the Yale farm.
Brooke Twombley	All this is very painful, Mater – what?

Lady Twombley	[*Crying*] What a silly woman I've been, Brooke!
Brooke Twombley	We're all thoughtless at times.
Lady Twombley	If I had but pulled in when pa's Irish rents began to dwindle!
Brooke Twombley	Why didn't you, Mater?
Lady Twombley	I don't know, but I didn't. I only prayed for better times and ordered Gillow to refurnish the dining-room. Last season I got through eighteen thousand pounds!
Brooke Twombley	Oh!

[LADY TWOMBLEY *twists round pointing to the walls of the conservatory*]

Lady Twombley	And look! Look at this sixpenny Algerian grotto I've stuck in the middle of the house. Seven thousand four hundred and fifty this cost, not counting the hot-water pipes.
Brooke Twombley	Is it paid for?
Lady Twombley	Your dear pa transferred the money for it to my account at Scott's, but I've gone and spent it on other things.
Brooke Twombley	Mater!
Lady Twombley	Oh, my poor heart!
Brooke Twombley	Well, Mater, any assistance I can render you in this emergency –
Lady Twombley	Ah, I know. [*Seizing his hand and kissing it*] My Brooke! My comfort!
Probyn	[*Outside*] Lady Drumdurris – Dowager Lady Drumdurris.
Brooke Twombley	Egidia and Aunt Dora.
Lady Twombley	[*Wiping her eyes*] Your aunt mustn't see me upset. Brooke, don't think any more of what I've told you. I've tumbled into the mud before now, but mud dries to dust and I've always managed to shake it off. Dora!

[*The* DOWAGER COUNTESS OF DRUMDURRIS *enters – a portly, rather formidable-looking lady of forty-five or fifty, in Court dress and diamonds*]

Well, Dora, are you tired?

Dowager	I hope I am never fatigued in doing my duty to my family, Kate. Here is poor Egidia.

[EGIDIA, COUNTESS OF DRUMDURRIS *enters – a small, serious girl, with a great deal of presence and dignity, also in Court dress*]

Egidia How do you do, Lady Twombley?

Lady Twombley Why, <u>poor</u> Egidia! Aren't you well, dear?

Dowager Egidia received a telegram from Scotland this morning; her son has cut his first tooth, during her absence, painfully.

Lady Twombley Oh, dear!

Egidia You also are a mother, Lady Twombley. You can sympathize with such cares as those I am now endeavouring to sustain.

[LADY EUPHEMIA *and* IMOGEN *stroll in*]

Lady Twombley Your boy is five months old, isn't he?

Egidia Fergus is precisely five months.

Lady Twombley Well, there are two-and-twenty more teeth to come yet, you know.

Egidia Yes, I am schooling myself into that conviction. I am naturally, I hope, a woman of more than ordinary courage.

[PROBYN *appears at the entrance*]

Probyn Lord Drumdurris.

[*The* EARL OF DRUMDURRIS, *a boyish-looking officer of the guards, in uniform, with much dignity and reserve, enters*]

Earl of Drumdurris How do you do, Lady Twombley? Egidia.

Dowager Keith, you have further news from Scotland?

Earl of Drumdurris Another telegram.

Egidia Ah!

[*She puts her hand calmly in that of the* DOWAGER]

Dowager Tell us, my son.

Earl of Drumdurris Another tooth. [EGIDIA *close her eyes. The* DOWAGER *kisses her upon the brow*] I offered Lady Macphail and Sir Colin the use of my brougham, but they preferred coming on here in their chariot.

Lady Twombley Lady Macphail and Sir Colin! Coming here!

Dowager	[*To* LADY TWOMBLEY] I haven't told you what I've done. Keith!
Earl of Drumdurris	[*Bowing*] Certainly.
	[*He joins the others who are talking together*]
Dowager	[*To* LADY TWOMBLEY] I have a motive. My whole life has been one vast comprehensive motive. Lady Macphail is the little woman to whom I introduced you on the stairs at the Palace.
Lady Twombley	Well, but –
Dowager	I encountered her again, and delivered a message from you begging her to come on here with Sir Colin to drink tea.
Lady Twombley	I never –
Dowager	I know you didn't. My motive is this. She has just brought her boy to London.
Lady Twombley	Is he the great man in the kilt I saw holding on to her lappets?
Dowager	Yes.
Lady Twombley	He's thirty, if he's an hour.
Dowager	He's more. But he is a fine example of the grand simplicity that exists in many Scottish families. Proprietor of eighty thousand acres, head of a great clan, Colin Macphail of Ballocheevin remains a child attached to his mother.
Lady Twombley	Oh, I shall be very happy to –
Dowager	Ah, you grasp my motive!
Lady Twombley	No, I don't!
Dowager	[*In* LADY TWOMBLEY*'s ear*] <u>Imogen</u>.
Lady Twombley	Imogen?
Dowager	Imogen <u>must</u> make a match this season and marry before the year is out.
Lady Twombley	Why?
Dowager	Don't deceive yourself, Kate Twombley. You are aware that Julian's position in the Ministry is precarious?
Lady Twombley	You think so?

Dowager	Everybody thinks so. It's my opinion they'll make a Jonah of him and cast him from them before many months are over. You know what that means?
Lady Twombley	Horrible! Julian giving up public life and settling down in some dismal swamp as a country gentleman. He has threatened it.
Dowager	Very well then; you must assure your children's future before the blow falls. What could you do for Imogen in the country?
Lady Twombley	A vicar or a small squire.
Dowager	More likely a curate or a farmer. Will you resign yourself to that?
Lady Twombley	Never, Dora! I never will! I've had to swallow the husks of London and my chicks shall have the barley. Julian <u>shall</u> hold on till they have made brilliant marriages!
Dowager	Ah!
Lady Twombley	He shall! Afterwards I'll go back to darning stockings with a light heart.
Dowager	Well spoken, Kate Twombley!
	[PROBYN *appears at the entrance*]
Probyn	Sir Colin and Lady Macphail.
Dowager	You see my motive?
Lady Twombley	Yes, Dora.
	[LADY MACPHAIL *and* SIR COLIN *enter – she a simple little old woman in Court dress, ecstatically sentimental; he a formidable-looking bearded man about six feet high, in full Highland costume, bashful and awkward in manner, and keeping close to his mother*]
	[*To* LADY MACPHAIL] I am delighted to see you here.
Lady Macphail	[*Presenting* MACPHAIL] My boy. [*He shelters himself behind her and bows uneasily*] I have determined to give the lad a season in this mighty city, Lady Twombley.
Lady Twombley	Ah, he'll enjoy himself, I'm sure.
Lady Macphail	Nay, the Macphails never enjoy themselves in the South.
Lady Twombley	I'm very sorry; perhaps they don't go the right way about it.

Lady Macphail	Already Colin's feet ache –
Lady Twombley	Do they?
Lady Macphail	Ache to press the heather again, searching for a sight of the red-deer in the misty chasms of Ben Muchty, or the wild birds fluttering on the gray shore of Loch-na-Doich.
Lady Twombley	Ah, very pretty country, I dare say.
Lady Macphail	Where would you be, Colin, at this hour at Castle Ballocheevin? Watching the sun sink behind the black peak of Ben-na-Vrachie? Speak, lad!
Macphail	[*Sadly*] That is so, mother.
Lady Twombley	Do you do that every evening at home?
Macphail	Aye.
Lady Macphail	Ah, a Macphail always feels like a seagull with a broken wing in the South.
Lady Twombley	You must take care you don't get him run over.
Probyn	[*Appearing at the entrance*] Tea is in the yellow room, my lady.

[DRUMDURRIS, BROOKE, EGIDIA, *and* LADY EUPHEMIA *go out*]

Dowager	[*Introducing* IMOGEN] Lady Macphail, Sir Colin – my niece, Imogen. Imogen, take Sir Colin to tea.
Imogen	This way, Sir Colin.
Dowager	[*To* LADY TWOMBLEY] You see my motive?
Imogen	[*Waiting for* MACPHAIL] Tea is in this room, Sir Colin.
Macphail	[*Looking at* IMOGEN, *and then, appealingly, at* LADY MACPHAIL] Come, mother.

[IMOGEN, MACPHAIL *and* LADY MACPHAIL *go out*]

| Dowager | [*To* LADY TWOMBLEY, *following the others*] He is impressed! |

[SIR JULIAN, *in evening dress, enters with a letter in his hand*]

Sir Julian Twombley	Katherine! Katherine!
Lady Twombley	Pa?
Sir Julian Twombley	I must speak to you.
Lady Twombley	But Dora has just brought a Highland youth here.
Sir Julian Twombley	I can't help it.

Lady Twombley	What's wrong, pa? How pale and waxy you look!
Sir Julian Twombley	[*Handing her the letter*] An urgent letter from old Mr Mason, my solicitor, about my affairs.
Lady Twombley	Oh, Lor', pa – another!
Sir Julian Twombley	You have it upside down.
Lady Twombley	Everything connected with our affairs <u>will</u> get that way.
Sir Julian Twombley	Mason is imperative.
Lady Twombley	He insists upon your considering your pecuniary position.
Sir Julian Twombley	What shall I do?
Lady Twombley	Accede to his request – consider it.
Sir Julian Twombley	But I am constantly considering it!
Lady Twombley	Hush, pa!
Sir Julian Twombley	No man's pecuniary position has ever demanded or received more consideration than my own. Day and night my pecuniary position lashes my brain into the consistency of a whipped egg.
Lady Twombley	Pa, be calm!
Sir Julian Twombley	Kate, my pecuniary position interposes between me and grave public questions. My very spectacles are toned by it. It is in every blue-book, in every page of Hansard, in the preamble of every Bill.
Lady Twombley	Oh, dear pa!
Sir Julian Twombley	It sits with me in committees, accompanies me into the lobbies; it receives deputations, replies to questions in the House; it forms part of the deliberations of the Cabinet. It warps my political sympathies; it distorts my judgement; it obscures my eloquence, and it lames my logic! [*Taking the letter from* LADY TWOMBLEY] And Mason – asks – me – to consider it!
	[*He leans his head on his hands. She sits on the arm of his chair*]
Lady Twombley	[*Tearfully*] Julian, you – mustn't – give way. Suppose the members of the Opposition saw you like this.
Sir Julian Twombley	[*With a groan*] Oh!

Lady Twombley	Think of those persons who sit – where is it? – on the hatchway – or below the gangway, or some uncomfortable place. How rejoiced they'd be! [*Shaking him gently*] Have courage, Julian – perk up, pa, dear.
Sir Julian Twombley	I cannot go on, Kitty.
Lady Twombley	Oh, don't say that!
Sir Julian Twombley	Mason's letter decides me.
Lady Twombley	To do what!
Sir Julian Twombley	Yield to sentiment which I have reason to believe exists on both sides of the House –
Lady Twombley	Resign?
Sir Julian Twombley	Resign my place in the Ministry – ask for the Chiltern Hundreds –
Lady Twombley	Oh!
Sir Julian Twombley	Wind up my affairs in town –
Lady Twombley	Oh, no!
Sir Julian Twombley	And seek peace in rural retirement.
Lady Twombley	You shan't, pa! Oh, my gracious, you wouldn't be so heartless!
Sir Julian Twombley	Heartless!
Lady Twombley	[*Kneeling beside him*] Think of my blessed chicks – my babies. Don't go under, Julian, till we've given them the benefit of our magnificent position –
Sir Julian Twombley	Our mag –
Lady Twombley	Wait till my Brooky – our Brooky – has won some handsome, wealthy girl who is worthy of him. Hold on till Imogen has made a marriage that will make every true mother's mouth water. Then I'll settle down with you alone, in a marsh. But don't sink into obscurity till the end of the year! I can do wonders by Christmas! Give me till then, pa – give me till then!
	[*She throws her arms round his neck.* IMOGEN's *harp is heard again.* MRS GAYLUSTRE *enters*]
Mrs Gaylustre	The wretches! How they ignore me! [*Seeing* SIR JULIAN *and* LADY TWOMBLEY] Ah!

[Hiding herself behind a pillar she listens]

Sir Julian Twombley	But – but – but if I desperately cling to public life a little longer I must have money.
Lady Twombley	Of course – of course you must have money. But, Julian, you must look to me for that.
Sir Julian Twombley	You Katherine!
Lady Twombley	You must think only of your value to the country, and – leave the rest to your wife.
Sir Julian Twombley	Kitty, you have made some little private hoard out of your allowance!
Lady Twombley	*[Sinking faintly onto the settee]* Well, pa.
Sir Julian Twombley	How prudent! How thoughtful!
Lady Twombley	Go – go to Dora. Make my excuses. I'll follow you when I've pulled myself together.
Sir Julian Twombley	Yes, yes. *[Turning]* By the way, Kitty, Hopwoods have just sent in their bill for erecting this conservatory.
Lady Twombley	*[Clinging to the back of the chair]* Oh!
Sir Julian Twombley	You remember I transferred, at your request, seven thousand some odd pounds to your account at Scott's when we projected the – h'm! – pardonable little extravagance.
Lady Twombley	Y-yes.
Sir Julian Twombley	Hopwoods can wait till midsummer. Perhaps you wouldn't mind letting me have use of the money in the meantime?
Lady Twombley	No, certainly not.
Sir Julian Twombley	A cheque any day this week –
Lady Twombley	All days are equally convenient.
Sir Julian Twombley	Kitty I <u>will</u> hold on till Christmas!
Lady Twombley	Thank you, pa – I – *[She turns to him suddenly]* Oh, pa, I haven't got – I haven't – I –
Sir Julian Twombley	Haven't what, Kitty?
Lady Twombley	N-nothing. Go – go to Dora. *[He goes out]* Oh! Where shall I turn for money? Where shall I turn? Where shall I turn – for money?

[MRS GAYLUSTRE *advances and faces* LADY TWOMBLEY]

Ah! Mrs Gaylustre!

Mrs Gaylustre	Oh, Lady Twombley, I am in such distress.
Lady Twombley	Distress!
Mrs Gaylustre	[*Producing* LADY TWOMBLEY's *letter to* BROOKE] I picked up a letter in the next room. I thought it was the note you wrote me about the plum-coloured *peignoir* and that it had fallen from my pocket. I glanced at it. Oh, look!

[*She hands the letter to* LADY TWOMBLEY]

Lady Twombley	Gracious!
Mrs Gaylustre	But that is not the worst. It tells m e that you are in trouble – you, the best friend I have in the world, my benefactress. Oh, what shall I do?
Lady Twombley	Hold your tongue about it.
Mrs Gaylustre	Ah! Why did I read it through?
Lady Twombley	Because you were a little curious, I'm afraid.
Mrs Gaylustre	I shan't sleep for it.
Lady Twombley	Thank you, I can do all my own lying awake. Mind your own concerns for the future, Gaylustre.
Mrs Gaylustre	It is my concern when I can help you.
Lady Twombley	You help me?
Mrs Gaylustre	Ah, yes. Oh, let me, Lady Twombley! I don't ask to be confided in, I only ask to be allowed to bring my brother to see you – tonight – tomorrow.
Lady Twombley	Your brother?
Mrs Gaylustre	Mr Lebanon – my Joseph. I would trust him as I'd trust myself. I have known him do such things in the way of raising money upon what he calls personal and other security –
Lady Twombley	A money-lender?
Mrs Gaylustre	Lady Twombley! Oh!
Lady Twombley	Does Mr Lebanon help – people – in difficulties?
Mrs Gaylustre	Oh, doesn't he!
Lady Twombley	Oh!

Mrs Gaylustre	Will you see him, Lady Twombley?
Lady Twombley	Don't ask me. Perhaps.
Mrs Gaylustre	Tonight?
Lady Twombley	Perhaps, I tell you.
Mrs Gaylustre	At what time?
Lady Twombley	Half past nine – sharp.
Mrs Gaylustre	[*To herself*] Done!

[SIR JULIAN *enters with* LADY MACPHAIL, MACPHAIL, *and the* DOWAGER. BROOKE *follows with* DRUMDURRIS, *then after an interval* LADY EUPHEMIA, EGIDIA *and* IMOGEN *appear*]

Sir Julian Twombley	[*To* LADY TWOMBLEY *reprovingly*] My dear, Lady Macphail and Sir Colin are going.
Dowager	[*To* LADY TWOMBLEY] You are neglecting them. What can be your motive?
Lady Twombley	[*To* LADY MACPHAIL] I hope Sir Julian has explained –
Lady Macphail	Certainly. But I must take my boy away. He dines at six to avoid late hours.

[IMOGEN *talks to* MACPHAIL]

Dowager	[*Quietly to* LADY TWOMBLEY] Look! They are talking.
Lady Macphail	Colin rises at five every morning.
Lady Twombley	Dear me, how awful!
Lady Macphail	He loves to watch the sunrise from the jagged summit of Ben-na-fechan.
Lady Twombley	But there's no Ben-na-what-you-may-call-it here.
Lady Macphail	No. But he sits upon the roof of our lodgings in Clarges Street. Good-bye, Lady Twombley.

[*They shake hands*]

Lady Twombley	[*To* MACPHAIL] Good-bye. You must come and see me on one of my Tuesdays.
Macphail	Aye, with my mother.

[*He turns to* IMOGEN; *they shake hands*]

Imogen	Good-bye, Sir Colin.
Dowager	[*To* LADY TWOMBLEY] There again! Look!

Brooke Twombley	Why, here's Valentine! Valentine!
Lady Twombley	[*Inquiringly*] Valentine?
	[BROOKE *brings on* VALENTINE]
Valentine White	[*To* BROOKE] Let me go! I was trying to find my way out.
Brooke Twombley	[*To* LADY TWOMBLEY] Here's Valentine, come back.
Imogen	Valentine!
Valentine White	Imogen!
Imogen	Oh, my dear Val! My dear old Val!
	[*She rushes to him impulsively and flings her arms round his neck, at which the* DOWAGER *gives a cry of horror, and there is a general movement of astonishment*]

End of the First Act

The Second Act

Difficulties

[*The scene is a handsomely decorated and elegantly furnished morning-room at* SIR JULIAN TWOMBLEY's, *with every evidence of luxury and refined taste. It is a July morning*]

[SIR JULIAN *is playing his flute.* MR MELTON, *a good-looking, well-dressed young man, enters carrying a few sheets of paper*]

Mr Melton Pardon me.

[SIR JULIAN's *flute gives a squeak*]

Sir Julian Twombley Oh, Melton?

Mr Melton The arrangements for this morning are quite complete, Sir Julian.

Sir Julian Twombley The arrangements?

Mr Melton The arrangements for the opening of the new street.

Sir Julian Twombley Oh, to be sure; I open the new street today. Why on earth shouldn't a new street be opened by a policeman during the night, quietly?

[*The* DOWAGER LADY DRUMDURRIS, *fashionably dressed for out-of-doors, enters*]

Dowager [*In a flutter*] Julian, good morning. A glorious day for the ceremony, Mr Melton. Is everything arranged?

Mr Melton [*Bowing*] Everything.

Dowager I have a motive for asking. I and my family accompany Sir Julian and Lady Twombley to lend weight and support.

Mr Melton [*To* SIR JULIAN] You leave here at twelve, reaching the new street at half-past. You speak from the cluster of lamps by St. Jude's church.

Dowager Your speech will be terse, elegant, and vigorous, I hope, Julian?

Sir Julian Twombley I hope so. Have you written it, Mr Melton? [MELTON *hands him the sheets of paper*] Thank you. The usual thing, I suppose?

Mr Melton	Quite, quite.
Sir Julian Twombley	Thank you. There's nothing like the usual thing. [*Referring to the speech*] "By opening up these majestic avenues London takes beer – "
Mr Melton	Air.
Sir Julian Twombley	I beg your pardon. " – takes air into her system and keeps her place in the race with her sister cities." Excellent.
Dowager	Who will throw the bottle?
Sir Julian Twombley	No-one, I hope.
Mr Melton	You are thinking of the christening of a ship, Lady Drumdurris.
Dowager	Pardon me.
Mr Melton	I have to see Superintendent Snudden now as to the police arrangements.
Sir Julian Twombley	Dear me! You anticipate no pellets?
Mr Melton	Hardly.
Sir Julian Twombley	It's so unfortunate it isn't a wet day.
Dowager	Julian!
Sir Julian Twombley	An umbrella is such a safeguard.
Mr Melton	I'll see that the carriage closes easily.
Sir Julian Twombley	Thank you. And Lady Twombley might take an extra sunshade.
	[MELTON *goes out. The* DOWAGER *closes the door carefully after him*]
	[*Reading*] "I can conceive no position more agreeable to a Minister of the Crown than that which – "
Dowager	Julian!
Sir Julian Twombley	Dora?
Dowager	You wonder why I am with you at this early hour. I need hardly say I have a motive.
Sir Julian Twombley	I suppose so.
Dowager	Knowing that you were not going down to Browning Street this morning, and that Lady Twombley and Imogen were to take Euphemia shopping in Bond Street, I grasped

	the chance of seeing you alone. Julian, what has happened to your wife?
Sir Julian Twombley	To Katherine?
Dowager	There is a shocking change.
Sir Julian Twombley	Recently?
Dowager	It began two or three months ago. She's not the woman she was at the commencement of the season.
Sir Julian Twombley	You alarm me. In what way?
Dowager	Every way. Her appearance.
Sir Julian Twombley	I haven't noticed it.
Dowager	Being her husband, it is natural you should not. Her variable temperament! At one moment she looks as if she would like to bury everybody, me especially; the next she is laughing in a manner I must designate as positively provincial.
Sir Julian Twombley	Dora, you quite distress me.
Dowager	I came early for that purpose.
Sir Julian Twombley	Thank you.
Dowager	Perhaps you resent my interference.
Sir Julian Twombley	No, no.
Dowager	It would not deter me if you did. The grand motive of my life is a firm, undeviating, persistent policy of practical interference. I am a social warrior; the moment I scent domestic carnage I hurl myself into the *mêlée* and plant my flag. Julian, my flag is planted in your household.
Sir Julian Twombley	But I am aware of nothing disquieting to Katherine's peace of mind.
Dowager	Don't tell me!
Sir Julian Twombley	Two or three months ago there <u>was</u> a little difficulty –
Dowager	Ah!
Sir Julian Twombley	But it was mine, not Katherine's.
Dowager	Yours?
Sir Julian Twombley	Frankly, I was embarrassed for ready money.
Dowager	Oh, dear!

Sir Julian Twombley	But Katherine, who is really of an extremely thrifty nature, promptly placed her very considerable savings at my disposal, and the difficulty eased.
Dowager	It never struck me your wife was thrifty.
Sir Julian Twombley	Nor me till that moment. Which shows how liable the most careful observer is to error. [*Resuming the study of his speech*] Pray excuse me.
Dowager	[*To herself*] Um! [*She goes up to the window*]
Sir Julian Twombley	[*Studying*] "I can conceive no position more agreeable to a Minister of the Crown – " I'll go upstairs quietly. " – than that which I occupy on this occasion."
	[*He moves softly towards the door. The* DOWAGER *turns suddenly*]
Dowager	Julian!
Sir Julian Twombley	Dora?
Dowager	I don't like your wife's great friendship for Mrs Gaylustre.
Sir Julian Twombley	Katherine finds her a bright companion.
Dowager	Katherine has <u>my</u> companionship. It's true I can't cut a sleeve like that lady.
Sir Julian Twombley	It is to be regretted that poor Mrs Gaylustre is forced to follow the modern fashion of increasing her income by devices formerly practised only by the lower middle-classes.
Dowager	She sticks pins in her bosom as though she relished it.
Sir Julian Twombley	But, after all, Dora, Madame Mauricette, of Plunkett Street, and Mrs Gaylustre, widow of Lord Bulpitt's son, are two very distinct persons. Excuse me.
	[*He continues studying his speech*]
Dowager	But what was she <u>before</u> her marriage?
Sir Julian Twombley	You must really give me notice of that question – I beg your pardon – I don't know.
Dowager	This lady now walks into your house as if it were her own!
Sir Julian Twombley	Ah!

Dowager	Your wife is positively canvassing for invitations for her! Julian!
Sir Julian Twombley	I shall be unprepared with my speech!
Dowager	My family comes before everything!
	[PROBYN *enters*]
Probyn	Lord and Lady Drumdurris are inquiring for you, my lady.
Dowager	Beg them to come here.
	[PROBYN *retires*]
Sir Julian Twombley	Ah, then, if you allow me –
Dowager	No, Julian. This is another family matter of terrible importance.
Sir Julian Twombley	My dear Dora!
Dowager	Keith and Egidia approach you at this early hour at my instigation. I have a painful motive.
Sir Julian Twombley	Oh, dear me!
	[EGIDIA *enters, dressed in fashionable walking costume, her face pale and troubled*]
Egidia	[*Sadly*] Sir Julian.
Sir Julian Twombley	My dear Egidia, there is nothing amiss, I hope?
Egidia	Ah! Everything is amiss, Sir Julian.
Dowager	Julian, the relations between my son and his wife have become terribly strained.
Sir Julian Twombley	No, no!
Egidia	Indeed, yes!
Dowager	I have done all in my power to relieve the horrible tension – if anything, I have made matters worse. My hope is now centred in you. Here is Keith.
Egidia	Ah!
	[EGIDIA *sits upon a settee staring before her.* DRUMDURRIS *enters, looking much worried*]
Earl of Drumdurris	Ah, mother. [*Grasping* SIR JULIAN's *hand with feeling*] Sir Julian.
	[DRUMDURRIS *and his wife look severely at each other and draw themselves up*]

Sir Julian Twombley	My dear Keith, what can I do for you?
Earl of Drumdurris	Ha! Explain, mother.
Dowager	Julian, my son and his wife have cordially agreed to refer their grave differences to your judgement.
Egidia	Without binding ourselves to abide by Sir Julian's decision.
Earl of Drumdurris	Naturally.
Sir Julian Twombley	Pray tell me the cause of dispute.
Dowager	The future of their child.
Egidia	Ah, yes.
Dowager	The adjustment of the career he is to follow.
Earl of Drumdurris	That is precisely it.
Dowager	[*To* DRUMDURRIS] Where is Fergus?
Earl of Drumdurris	He accompanied us.
Egidia	He is with Angèle in the next room.
Dowager	[*Calling at the door*] Angèle! Angèle!
Angèle	[*Outside*] Miladi?
Dowager	Bring Lord Aberbrothock here.
	[ANGÈLE, *a French nurse, characteristically attired, enters, carrying a richly-dressed infant.* DRUMDURRIS *and* EGIDIA *look into its face together*]
Angèle	Figurez-vous, milord, qu'il a dormi pendant tout le trajet! Et puis quand je suis descendue de voiture, il s'est reveillé en pleurant . . . ah mais, en pleurant!
Dowager	Give me Lord Aberbrothock. [*She takes the child from* ANGÈLE] Wait in the next room, Angèle.
Angèle	Yes, miladi. J'espère bien que Monsieur le Vicomte ne vas plus crier, car ça pourrait faire de la peine à sa grand'maman. [ANGÈLE *goes out*]
Dowager	Now, Julian, this is the point. You see Fergus. Politics or the Army?
Egidia	Politics.
Earl of Drumdurris	The Army.

Dowager	Pray speak, Julian.
Sir Julian Twombley	Er – um – perhaps it would be rather precipitate –
Egidia	I differ entirely. The child's intelligence must be directed into a particular channel from the beginning.
Earl of Drumdurris	In that I heartily concur. For instance, the question of toys is already most urgent.
Egidia	He is without playthings at present, so his mind is quite open.
Dowager	You appear to have no views, Julian.
Egidia	Lady Drumdurris, let Sir Julian look at the height and character of Fergus's brow.
Earl of Drumdurris	Pray do. It's a soldier's forehead.
Dowager	Julian.
	[*She hands the infant to* SIR JULIAN]
Sir Julian Twombley	Thank you. Politics or the Army? [*Addressing the child in his arms*] My dear Fergus, take my advice, not, <u>not</u> politics.
Egidia	Ah!
Sir Julian Twombley	If you attach any trifling importance to veracity as a habit, <u>not</u> politics. If you would care at any time upon any subject to form your own opinions, and having formed them, would wish to maintain them, <u>not</u> politics. If you desire to be of the smallest service to your fellow man, and if you would sleep as peacefully at sixty as you now sleep at six months, <u>not</u> politics.
Egidia	Sir Julian!
Earl of Drumdurris	The Army!
Egidia	Never!
Dowager	This is most distressing. [*Calling at the open door*] Angèle! Angèle!
Lady Twombley	[*Heard outside*] Why, Dora!
Sir Julian Twombley	Katherine.
	[LADY TWOMBLEY *enters with* IMOGEN *and* LADY EUPHEMIA *in walking costumes*]

Lady Twombley	How good of you come early! [*Kissing* EGIDIA] Egidia, dearest! [*To* DRUMDURRIS] Good-morning, Keith. Ah! You've brought Fergus to see me! The angel!
	[*With cries of delight* LADY TWOMBLEY, IMOGEN, *and* LADY EUPHEMIA *gather round* SIR JULIAN *and the baby*]
	The pet!
Imogen	The mite!
Lady Euphemia Vibart	He is <u>too</u> sweet!
The Three	Oh-h-h!
	[BROOKE *enters*]
Brooke Twombley	[*Shaking hands with* DRUMDURRIS] Hallo, what's the matter?
Earl of Drumdurris	[*With dignity*] They are looking at my son.
	[ANGÈLE *has entered. She takes the infant from* SIR JULIAN]
Lady Twombley	We've enjoyed a splendid hour in Bond Street — in and out of twenty shops, eh, girls?
Lady Euphemia Vibart	Yes, Aunt Kate.
Imogen	Yes, mamma.
Lady Twombley	Bought all we could think of and ordered the rest.
Sir Julian Twombley	My dear!
Lady Twombley	Then why don't they abolish Bond Street? It's the crucible of London — set foot in it and everything about you that's metal dissolves.
Lady Euphemia Vibart	Aunt has been <u>too</u> extravagant this morning.
Lady Twombley	Extravagant! I! Oh, no — only I dearly wish there was no such plague as money. If the little words "thank you" were one universal current coin, what anxieties, what cravings, what follies some poor women could be spared! Why can't we buy choice stuffs at three-and-a-half thank-yous a yard?
Lady Euphemia Vibart	Oh, Aunt Kate!
Imogen	Mamma!
Lady Twombley	It's nothing to laugh at. Ah, girls, if "thank you" paid for everything, being out of breath would be our only bankruptcy! Oh, my poor brain!

Imogen	[*To* SIR JULIAN] Mamma has a bad headache today, papa.
Lady Twombley	A headache! Never! Girls, what is it we bought and brought home with us? I forget.
Imogen	We didn't buy him, mamma – we met him. You mean Cousin Valentine.
Lady Twombley	[*Looking around*] Of course – Valentine. Where is he? [*Calling*] Valentine!
	[VALENTINE *enters very plainly dressed*]
Sir Julian Twombley	Mr White! [*Bowing stiffly*] How do you do?
Brooke Twombley	Why, Val! What?
Lady Twombley	We met the poor boy outside the tourists' ticket office in Piccadilly. He's off again tomorrow.
Brooke Twombley	Off! Where to?
Valentine White	Egypt.
Lady Twombley	We shan't see him again for another ten years, I suppose.
Imogen	Oh, mamma!
Lady Twombley	The odd creature has heard of a congenial tribe who reside in excavations cut in a rock. It'll end in my having a nephew who's a mummy.
Imogen	[*Tearfully*] Oh, don't!
Sir Julian Twombley	Katherine, this child is not well.
Imogen	Yes, I am, papa – but I don't like – the idea – of parting – with anybody or anything – even a k-k-kitten.
Lady Twombley	[*Soothingly*] Imogen, my dear!
Imogen	Be quiet, mamma!
	[*The* DOWAGER, LADY EUPHEMIA, EGIDIA *and* ANGÈLE *with the baby go out.* IMOGEN *runs after them.* SIR JULIAN *resumes the study of his speech.* LADY TWOMBLEY *opens some letters which are lying on the table*]
Brooke Twombley	[*To* VALENTINE] I never knew such a queer chap! Come upstairs and tell us about it – what!
	[BROOKE, VALENTINE, *and* DRUMDURRIS *go out*]
Lady Twombley	Oh!
Sir Julian Twombley	Katherine?

Lady Twombley	It's all right, pa – it's nothing. [*To herself*] Gaylustre! [*Reading a letter*] "I will accompany you and dear Sir Julian to the interesting ceremony of this morning. Pray keep me a seat in your carriage." [*Crushing the letter in her hand*] The demon! The relentless demon!
Sir Julian Twombley	"I can conceive no position more agreeable to a Minister of the Crown -"
Lady Twombley	Pa, Mrs Gaylustre will go with us to the opening of the new street.
Sir Julian Twombley	H'm! Katherine, are you sure that Mrs Gaylustre is quite –
Lady Twombley	Oh, quite.
Sir Julian Twombley	If I were you I should really think twice –
Lady Twombley	Oh, I can't.
Sir Julian Twombley	Can't think twice?
Lady Twombley	I can't risk offending such a – dear friend.
Sir Julian Twombley	But, Katherine –
Lady Twombley	Understand me, pa – she will sit in our carriage.
Sir Julian Twombley	Then understand me, Katherine, I will not have my knees cramped by a lady whose social status is equivocal.
Lady Twombley	Ah! Julian! Don't attempt to come between me and Mrs Gaylustre.
Sir Julian Twombley	Katherine!
Lady Twombley	You will assist her into the carriage, you will help her to alight; when she arrives you will be charmed to see her, when she leaves you will be a mass of regret. You hear me!
Sir Julian Twombley	This is a most extraordinary friendship!
Lady Twombley	It is an exceptional friendship. Pa, say you're delighted this great friend of mine is to be one of us today.
Sir Julian Twombley	Well, to please you, my dear, of course, I –
Lady Twombley	Yes?
Sir Julian Twombley	I am delighted.
Lady Twombley	Ah!

Sir Julian Twombley	[*To himself*] I see – I see the change in my wife that Dora spoke of.
	[PROBYN *enters with cards on a salver. At the same moment the* DOWAGER *enters and looks out of the window*]
Dowager	[*To herself*] They are punctual!
Lady Twombley	[*Looking at the cards*] Lady Macphail and Sir Colin. Not at home. If ever a woman was out I am.
Dowager	[*To* PROBYN] Stop! [*To* LADY TWOMBLEY] Kate, what are you doing? This visit is planned by me!
Lady Twombley	Why?
Dowager	I have a motive.
Lady Twombley	Oh, Dora!
Dowager	[*To* PROBYN] Lady Twombley will see Sir Colin and Lady Macphail here.
	[PROBYN *goes out*]
Sir Julian Twombley	Ah! Then if you'll allow me –
Dowager	No, Julian. This is another family matter.
Sir Julian Twombley	Another!
Dowager	These people have called to formally propose for the hand of Imogen.
Lady Twombley	To propose!
Dowager	Last night, at the ball of the Perth Highlanders, I danced the Strathspey and Reel with Sir Colin. In the excitement I wrung from him an admission of his affection.
Lady Twombley	Pa, what shall we do?
Dowager	Do? The head of the Clan Macphail! Eighty thousand acres! Julian?
Lady Twombley	[*To herself*] If it would provide for Imogen before the smash!
Dowager	If Imogen is a high-minded girl she will be mad with delight.
Lady Twombley	Will she? [*To herself*] Ah! And will she learn to look down on pa and me when we're aged paupers?
	[PROBYN *enters*]

Probyn	Sir Colin Macphail – Lady Macphail.
	[LADY MACPHAIL *enters, dressed simply and quaintly in an old-fashioned silk gown, followed closely by* MACPHAIL, *whose clothes are capacious and clumsy, and who seems very ill at ease.* PROBYN *withdraws*]
Dowager	Dear Lady Macphail – Sir Colin!
Lady Twombley	[*Shaking hands with* LADY MACPHAIL *and* MACPHAIL] How do you do? [*Eyeing* MACPHAIL] Oh, dear!
Sir Julian Twombley	[*Shaking hands*] Delighted.
Lady Twombley	[*To* MACPHAIL] Pray sit down. You must be fatigued with last night's dance.
Lady Macphail	No Macphail is ever fatigued. But the poor lad feels like a caged eagle in the dress of the South.
Lady Twombley	I am sure it is – most becoming.
Lady Macphail	Sit, lad.
	[MACPHAIL *sits, hitching up his trousers unhappily*]
	You know the object of our visit, Sir Julian?
Sir Julian Twombley	Lady Drumdurris has hinted –
Lady Macphail	The boy is here to pour out the passionate torrent of his love for your child, Imogen. Speak, Colin.
	[MACPHAIL *rouses himself, rises, and looks round*]
Macphail	Mother, you do it.
	[*He resumes his seat*]
Lady Macphail	Ah, if we were at Castle Ballocheevin, with the wind roaring round Ben Muchty, and the sound of pipers playing by the shores of Loch-na-Doich, then you would hear Colin's voice rise loud and high.
Sir Julian Twombley	As we are denied these obvious advantages, it is almost necessary to ask you to explain –
Lady Macphail	The lad has met your child on but three or four occasions.
Macphail	Just three occasions and a bit, Mother.
Lady Macphail	But he loves her with a love that only a Macphail can experience.
Lady Twombley	Of course one would like to know precisely the kind of affection that is.

Lady Macphail	Naturally. Speak, Colin.
	[MACPHAIL *rises, embarrassed*]
Macphail	I love her well enough.
Lady Macphail	Bravely said!
Dowager	Delightful [*To* SIR JULIAN *and* LADY MACPHAIL] A grand nature.
Lady Macphail	Go on, Colin.
Macphail	That's all, mother.
	[*He resumes his seat*]
Lady Macphail	[*To* LADY TWOMBLEY] You have heard the lad?
Lady Twombley	Distinctly.
Lady Macphail	As we are all to meet next month as Lord Drumdurris's guests at Drumdurris Castle, it would be well if this engagement were settled at once.
Dowager	Without delay.
Sir Julian Twombley	The question, of course, is whether Imogen – h'm!
Lady Twombley	Whether Imogen can return the affection –
Sir Julian Twombley	Which Sir Colin honours her by entertaining.
Lady Macphail	Has the lad your permission to pour into her ear such impassioned words as he has just uttered to us?
Lady Twombley	I think there can be no objection to <u>that</u>.
Dowager	Certainly not.
Lady Macphail	When will your daughter grant him an hour for that purpose?
Lady Twombley	An <u>hour</u>?
Macphail	Three-quarters will be enough, mother.
Lady Macphail	Bravely said!
Dowager	Charming!
Lady Twombley	When, Julian?
Sir Julian Twombley	H'm! When?
Dowager	When?
	[IMOGEN'*s voice is heard outside*]

Imogen	[*Calling*] Mamma, dear!
Dowager	When? I suggest now. Here is Imogen.

[MACPHAIL *rises hastily and awkwardly.* IMOGEN *enters*]

Imogen	Oh, I didn't know you had visitors. [*Shaking hands with* SIR COLIN *and* LADY MACPHAIL] Sir Colin – Lady Macphail.
Dowager	Now, Julian, leave them together! Katherine!
Sir Julian Twombley	Imogen, my dear.

[IMOGEN *comes to* SIR JULIAN. LADY TWOMBLEY, *the* DOWAGER, LADY MACPHAIL, *and* MACPHAIL *talk together*]

Talk to Sir Colin for a few moments while I look through my speech.

Imogen	Certainly, papa. [SIR JULIAN *goes out*] What an awful task! [*Taking a book from the table*]
Lady Macphail	[*Quietly to* MACPHAIL] Colin, let her hear how a Macphail can love. [*Kissing him*] My boy! [*To the* DOWAGER *and* LADY TWOMBLEY] I'll drive round to Lady Macwhirter's and return. Leave them! Ah, the pipers shall play to the home-coming of a bride at Castle Ballocheevin!

[*She goes out*]

Dowager	Come. Katherine. Think of it! To be the mother-in-law of the head of the Clan Macphail!
Lady Twombley	Dora, what's the use of a head with no tongue in it?

[*The* DOWAGER *and* LADY TWOMBLEY *go out.* MACPHAIL *looks round uneasily*]

Macphail	[*To himself*] Where's mother?
Imogen	[*To herself*] Oh, why do they leave us! [*To* MACPHAIL] Were you at the dance of the Perth Highlanders last night, Sir Colin?
Macphail	Aye, I was.
Imogen	Did you dance much?
Macphail	Aye, I did.
Imogen	[*To herself*] He must make the next remark.
Macphail	[*Nerving himself and rising suddenly*] Miss Twombley!
Imogen	Sir Colin!

TERMS AND CONDITIONS OF DEALING
STOCK EXCHANGE INVESTMENTS AND UNIT TRUSTS

National Westminster Bank PLC

1. The Bank may without prior reference to you effect transactions with or for you in which it has directly or indirectly a material interest or relationship of any description with another party which may involve a conflict with the Bank's duty to you.

2. All dealing will be subject to and in accordance with the rules and regulations of The Stock Exchange. Transactions will be effected through NatWest Stockbrokers Limited (the Stockbroker).

3. The Bank will not be bound to purchase any securities or units on your behalf unless it is satisfied that you are in funds to complete the transaction and also as to the authenticity of your instructions. Where the Bank is not so satisfied it may close out any transaction commenced and you will remain liable for any costs or expenses incurred by the Bank.

4. The Bank will not be bound to sell any securities or units on your behalf unless it is satisfied that you have title to such securities or units and also as to the authenticity of your instructions. If the Bank is not so satisfied it may close out any transaction undertaken on your behalf and you will remain liable for any costs or expenses incurred by the Bank.

5. The Bank shall not be liable for loss damage or delay however caused except where caused by the negligence or wilful default of the Bank or its employees or agents. All documents sent by post are sent at your risk.

6. The Bank may be charged a fee and expenses (at the rate prevailing at the time of the transaction) for dealing in investments which will be passed on to you and may receive back a portion of the fee as a commission (for which it shall not be required to account to you) for passing the instructions to the Stockbroker. These may change from time to time (without notice) and are additional to any charges payable on your banking account in relation to the transaction. Details of current charges are available on request from each Branch of the Bank.

7. Any fees charges or expenses will either be added to the purchase costs before entries are debited to your account, or deducted from sales proceeds before entries are credited to your account, as appropriate.

8. Confirmation of the execution of your instructions will be by way of a contract note or similar document of confirmation issued. Registered investments will be registered in your name unless otherwise instructed.

9. Where you give instructions to purchase units in a Regulated Collective Investment Scheme you will have no right under the Financial Services (Cancellation) Regulations 1987 to cancel the transaction.

10. All documents of title to any investments bought pursuant hereto will be held by the Branch on your behalf unless you instruct the Bank in writing to the contrary, and will be deemed to have been delivered to you as soon as they come into the possession of the Bank.

11. The Bank may disclose or permit disclosure of any information arising in connection with this transaction to any relevant authority or as required by such authority (whether or not pursuant to compulsion of law) and the Bank shall not be under any liability for any disclosure made in good faith by the Bank believing it to be in accordance with any such requirement.

12. You are advised that, if the transaction relates to a security issued by a company currently involved in a takeover situation, you **may be** obliged to report the transaction to The Stock Exchange.

13. If you are employed by a Regulated Investment Business you may require their prior permission to execute transactions.

14. The Bank may vary these Terms and Conditions from time to time upon giving notice by whatever means it deems fit.

15. If any advice is required on investments you will need to enter into a Customer Agreement with the Bank.

Macphail	I — I just wish you had been there.
Imogen	Do you? Why?
Macphail	Because — because I'm thinking there was room for more people.
Imogen	Oh, of course. [*She goes to the window and looks out*] Lady Macphail is just driving away.
Macphail	No!
Imogen	Yes, there she goes.
	[MACPHAIL *goes hastily to the window and looks out*]
Macphail	[*To himself*] Oh! Mother!
	[*He goes out quickly unnoticed by* IMOGEN]
Imogen	She has turned the corner, Sir Colin. Did you see her? Why, where is he?
	[VALENTINE *enters. She does not see him*]
Valentine White	Good-bye, Imogen.
	[*She turns to him*]
Imogen	Ah! [*Falteringly*] Why will you go away, Val?
Valentine White	You know my craze. Everything in this country is so stuck up.
Imogen	Mamma's not — stuck up, as you call it.
Valentine White	Her gowns frighten me. My first recollection of anything is Aunt Kitty in a print-skirt at a washtub.
Imogen	Hush! Don't, Val!
Valentine White	There now! You're horrified!
Imogen	One doesn't wish everybody to know.
Valentine White	Then that's being stuck up, Imogen.
Imogen	Then we differ.
Valentine White	Of course. Everybody does differ from me in this stuck up country. Wish me good-bye.
Imogen	[*Looking away*] I presume my brother, Brooke, is stuck up also?
Valentine White	Well, he appears to have fallen into the starch after that wash of Aunt Kitty's.

Imogen	Indeed. And, papa?
Valentine White	Oh, of course, he's ironed out by the House of Commons.
Imogen	How very rude! [*Laying her hand on his arm*] And am I – altered, Val?
Valentine White	Altered! The change is heart-breaking!
Imogen	Oh, how cruel!
Valentine White	Altered! Where are the tiny tea-things with which you once played at making tea in your old school-room? Where is the hoop you used to trundle in Portman Square – the skipping-rope Brooke and I turned for you till our arms nearly dropped from our shoulders? Where are the marbles I gave you – the top I taught you to spin? I say, where are these things and the jolly little girl who delighted in them?
Imogen	[*With much dignity*] I think you're so violent that it isn't safe to speak to you. But I'll ask you one question.
Valentine White	Pray do.
Imogen	Where is the good-tempered, curly-headed boy for whom I used to make the tea; the boy who taught me, very patiently, how to play the marbles and to spin the top?
Valentine White	You see him.
Imogen	Oh, no. No, Val, no.
Valentine White	Imogen! You don't mean, at any rate, that I'm stuck up?
Imogen	No, indeed, I think you're shockingly stuck down.
	[*He turns away, hanging his head. She comes to him*]
	There, now I've made you ashamed of yourself.
Valentine White	No, you haven't!
Imogen	Then I will do so. Remain here. I will return in a moment. Don't stir!
	[*She runs out*]
Valentine White	Shall I run away? Ah, if she only knew how ardently I wish that she had changed still more – how I wish that she had grown quite unlovable or I had forgotten how to love her! It's hopeless; I <u>will</u> run away.

[He opens the door and the DOWAGER *peeps in]*

Dowager May I come in?

Valentine White Eh? Oh, certainly.

[The DOWAGER *enters]*

Dowager *[To herself]* What has become of them? *[To* VALENTINE] Pardon me, have you seen my niece, Imogen?

Valentine White She has just left this room.

Dowager With Sir Colin Macphail?

Valentine White Oh, no.

[A cab whistle is heard. VALENTINE *looks out of the window]*

Dowager *[To herself]* Where is he? I shan't sleep till I know it is settled.

Valentine White Here's Sir Colin – hailing a cab.

Dowager Ah! Something must have happened! *[She goes hastily towards the door;* VALENTINE *is in her way]* Let me pass, please! I have a motive!

[She goes out as IMOGEN *enters by another door carrying a large old-fashioned box]*

Imogen Valentine.

Valentine White Why, what have you there?

Imogen A modern young lady's jewel casket. Open it, please.

[Kneeling, he opens the box]

Valentine White *[Looking into the box]* Imogen! The tea-things! I recognise them!

Imogen You see, I've never parted with my playthings, Val.

Valentine White *[Dragging out a large, faded, once gaudy doll]* And here's Rosa! I helped to cut out Rosa's mantle. Battered old Rosa!

Imogen *[Taking the doll from him]* Don't! Old she may be, but her sex should prevent her from insult.

Valentine White And here are my marbles! And the top! Ah, ah! The skipping-rope! Imogen – perhaps – I – I've done you an injustice.

Imogen Do you think so?

Valentine White	I feared fashion had put your bright little nature into tight corsets – but – I see – I see –
Imogen	[*Replacing the toys in the box*] You see, Val.
Valentine White	I see you have some affection for the time when you were not Miss Twombley, but only – little Jenny.
Imogen	Ah!
Valentine White	Not that these old dumb things prove much.
Imogen	Oh, Val!
Valentine White	They prove their own existence – not the existence of little Jenny.
Imogen	[*Crying*] How unjust you are!
Valentine White	Perhaps. But your words and actions are so unlike . . .
Imogen	[*Wiping her eyes upon the doll's frock*] No, no.
Valentine White	I fancy we are children again when I hear you; but when I see your prim figure and stately walk I miss the little girl whose hair never submitted to a ribbon or a hairpin –
Imogen	Oh!
	[*Impulsively she lets down her hair and disorders it wildly*]
Valentine White	[*Not observing her*] I miss little Jenny with a tumbled frock [*She quickly disarranges her bow and sash*], the thoughtless romp who was generally minus one shoe!
Imogen	[*Fiercely*] Valentine!
	[*She takes of a shoe and flings it away*]
Valentine White	Jenny!
Imogen	Now! Play! Play marbles!
Valentine White	What!
Imogen	Play marbles!
	[*They go down upon their knees, she deliberately arranges the marbles for the game, he staring at her blankly*]
	My mark – play.
Valentine White	I beg your pardon, Jenny – I've been all wrong.
Imogen	You have indeed, Val. Play. [*He plays seriously*] Not within a mile of it.

Valentine White	My eye is quite out.
Imogen	My turn.
Valentine White	By Jupiter, you're still a crack at it!
Imogen	Am I? Then which of us has changed – you or I? [*She lays her hand on his*] Val, don't go away and live in a rock.
Valentine White	What am I to do? I'm poor, Jenny, and I suppose I'm crazy.
Imogen	Any sort of horrid life would suit you, wouldn't it?
Valentine White	I suppose it would.
Imogen	Then ask Lord Drumdurris to make you a bailiff or a head gamekeeper at Drumdurris.
Valentine White	Not rough enough.
Imogen	Why, you could get dreadfully dirty and wet through there every day.
Valentine White	That's true.
Imogen	And, Val, we're all going up to Drumdurris next month.
Valentine White	Are you?
Imogen	Yes, and if you like, I – I'll bring the marbles.
	[BROOKE *enters*]
Brooke Twombley	Imogen! Oh, I say! What?
Valentine White	Do you ever play marbles now, Brooke?
	[DRUMDURRIS *enters*]
Brooke Twombley	Marbles, no! Billiards.
	[VALENTINE *collects the marbles and puts them into the box*]
Imogen	[*To* DRUMDURRIS] Keith! Oh, Keith, do me a favour!
Earl of Drumdurris	Certainly.
Imogen	Offer my poor cousin, Mr White, some post in or about Drumdurris Castle.
Earl of Drumdurris	What kind of post?
Imogen	Some wretched, inferior position in which he needn't be very polite.
Earl of Drumdurris	What will he say if I propose such a thing?
Imogen	He'll be extremely rude, I think. But, oh, I shall be so grateful, Keith.

[LADY TWOMBLEY enters]

Lady Twombley Imogen! Child, what has happened to your head?

Imogen I – I've been playing marbles, mamma.

Lady Twombley Not on your head?

Imogen No, mamma, upon the floor.

Lady Twombley With Sir Colin?

Imogen *[Putting up her hair]* Certainly not, mamma; I don't know Sir Colin nearly well enough to sit with him upon the floor.

Lady Twombley Darling, has Sir Colin made any remark of an interesting nature?

Imogen No – he stammered a little, and, while my back was turned, he ran away with his mammy.

Lady Twombley *[To herself]* I knew it! Why didn't we lock him in till he had provided for my poor child's future?

[PROBYN enters]

Probyn Mrs Gaylustre is here, my lady.

Imogen Oh, that person!

[IMOGEN snatches up the box of playthings and hurries out. MRS GAYLUSTRE enters. PROBYN retires]

Mrs Gaylustre *[To everybody]* How d'ye do? How d'ye do? Lord Drumdurris, charmed to see you. How are you, Brooke?

Brooke Twombley *[To himself]* Brooke! Impudence!

Mrs Gaylustre You look bilious, Kate.

[She kisses LADY TWOMBLEY, who sinks onto the settee]

Brooke Twombley *[To DRUMDURRIS]* It's too bad of the Mater! Fancy a fellow making a chum of his tailor – what?

Earl of Drumdurris Mr White, may I speak to you?

[BROOKE, DRUMDURRIS and VALENTINE go out]

Mrs Gaylustre *[Examining the flute]* Pa has been tootling again, Kate – we must buy him a drum.

Lady Twombley Ah-h-h-h!

Mrs Gaylustre Hullo! What's the matter?

Lady Twombley	As if you didn't know! Oh, those awful bits of paper!
Mrs Gaylustre	Still worrying about those little Bills of yours which my brother Joseph holds, eh?
Lady Twombley	Those Bills! Why doesn't the ink fade that's on them, or the house burn that holds 'em?
Mrs Gaylustre	Impossible. Joseph and I have been taught to believe that there is a special providence watching over all Bills of Exchange. Come, don't fume – Bill Number One doesn't fall due till next month.
Lady Twombley	Oh, Gaylustre, I shan't be able to meet it.
Mrs Gaylustre	Shan't you? Well, I dare say Jo and I will renew – if you make much of us and pet us. Meanwhile, don't think of the Bills.
Lady Twombley	Think of 'em! I eat them – they're on every <u>menu</u> – I drink them – they label the champagne. My pillows are stuffed with them, for I hear them rustle when I turn my restless head. Small as those strips of blue are, they paper every wall of my home!
Mrs Gaylustre	I should drive out, then, as much as possible.
Lady Twombley	When I do the sky is blue!
Mrs Gaylustre	[*Carelessly taking up a newspaper*] At what time do we leave here?
Lady Twombley	Sir Julian and I start at twelve.
Mrs Gaylustre	See that I'm not squeezed up in the carriage. I don't play at sardines in this gown.
Lady Twombley	Oh!
Mrs Gaylustre	Talking of sardines, I shall lunch here today, *en famille*.
Lady Twombley	Gaylustre! You fiend! I – I can't stand it!
Mrs Gaylustre	Don't quite see how you're going to get out of it.
Lady Twombley	It's true I owe that brother of yours thousands.
Mrs Gaylustre	Well, we <u>have</u> kept your establishment going for some time.
Lady Twombley	But I don't owe <u>you</u> as much as a linen button!
Mrs Gaylustre	Jo and I are one.

Lady Twombley	No! I'll never believe that a man – even a money-lender – would dance a set of devilish quadrilles on a lady when she's down, as you're doing.
Mrs Gaylustre	Ha, ha!
Lady Twombley	I saw your brother on that one fatal night. Common person that he is, he must have a heart under his vulgar waistcoat.
Mrs Gaylustre	Be careful! Don't insult my Jo!
Lady Twombley	I compliment him! I will appeal to him to protect me from your claws, Gaylustre!
Mrs Gaylustre	Oh, you will, will you?
Lady Twombley	I will.
Mrs Gaylustre	Very well then – do it! Kate Twombley, go to that door and call my brother Jo!
Lady Twombley	What!
Mrs Gaylustre	Do it!
Lady Twombley	What – do you – mean?
Mrs Gaylustre	Open that door and call Jo!
Lady Twombley	No, no! [*She opens the door and looks out*] You are only frightening me!
Mrs Gaylustre	Call – Mr Lebanon!
Lady Twombley	Mr Lebanon!
Mr Joseph Lebanon	[*Outside*] Heah!
	[LADY TWOMBLEY *utters a cry of horror as* MR JOSEPH LEBANON *enters – a smartly dressed, unctuous, middle-aged person, of a most pronounced common Semitic type, with a bland manner and a contented smile*]
	Lady Twombley, delighted to find myself in your elegant 'ouse. Most *recherché*.
Lady Twombley	How do you come here?
Mr Joseph Lebanon	Fan brought me.
Lady Twombley	How dare she?
Mr Joseph Lebanon	'Ow dare she? H'm! Fan, I 'ope and trust not a coolness between you and Lady T.

[LADY TWOMBLEY *sinks into a chair*]

Mrs Gaylustre	She was dying to see you – there's no pleasing her.
Mr Joseph Lebanon	Dyin' to see me! Flattered – flattered. [*He sits in close proximity to* LADY TWOMBLEY] Deah Lady T, you and I and nobody by, eh? Excuse my humour. 'Ow can I 'ave the honour of servin' you? Don't 'esitate, Lady T, don't 'esitate.
Lady Twombley	I only wanted – to beg you – to rid me of that viper.
Mrs Gaylustre	That's going a little too far!
Mr Joseph Lebanon	There is a coolness – a triflin', temporary coolness. Fan, be reasonable – Lady T, be forgivin'. Kiss and be friends.
Lady Twombley	I know that you've got me – what's the expression? – on something or another.
Mr Joseph Lebanon	I 'ope "toast" is not the word you requiah, Lady Twombley?
Lady Twombley	Oh, yes, on toast.
Mr Joseph Lebanon	Oh, Lady T! Lady T!
Lady Twombley	I know that if I can't meet those awful Bills you can drag my name into the papers, and set all London grinning for a month.
Mr Joseph Lebanon	Oh! Oh, Fan, is that the way of doin' business?
Lady Twombley	If you're a nice, honest, man – as you look – you'll take her away, and never, either of you, show your ugl – show your faces here again.
Mr Joseph Lebanon	Ah, Lady T, now we come to the aim and object of the mornin' call which I have the 'appiness of making on you. Fan, you haven't explained to Lady T. You really must cut in.
Mrs Gaylustre	I shan't. Explain yourself.

[LEBANON *rises, replacing his chair*]

Mr Joseph Lebanon	My dear Lady T, the long and the short of it is that Fan and I have considerable social ambition.
Lady Twombley	You too! Not you!
Mr Joseph Lebanon	And why not? Fanny, cut in!
Mrs Gaylustre	Go on, Jo, dear.

Mr Joseph Lebanon	Lady Twombley, it has been the desiah of Fan and self, ever since that period of our lives which I may describe as our checkered child'ood, to reach the top of the social tree.
Lady Twombley	Hah!
Mr Joseph Lebanon	Lady Twombley, you'll pardon my remarking that you are a little trying. I say, Fan and I desiah to reach the top of the social tree, where the cocoanuts are. Excuse my humour. Fan's had a whirl or two in the circles of fashion.
Lady Twombley	She! A hanger-on to the skirts of Society!
Mr Joseph Lebanon	And very good skirts too when she makes 'em.
Mrs Gaylustre	Jo, drop that.
Mr Joseph Lebanon	Excuse my humour, Fan. As for me, from those early boy'ood's days when I made temporary advances of ha'pence to my sister Fanny, promptly and without inquiry, I have devoted myself to finance.
Lady Twombley	Finance!
Mr Joseph Lebanon	But now, Lady T – to use a poetic figure – I am prepared to cut an eight on the frozen lake of gentility.
Lady Twombley	Man!
Mr Joseph Lebanon	I ignore the innuendo. Lady Twombley, I am aware that for a successful *entrée* into Society I requiah a – ha – a substantial guarantee. I 'ave, therefore, the honour and the 'appiness to put myself under your sheltering and I 'ope sympathetic wing.
Lady Twombley	You – you will drive me mad! You won't dare to call here, to contaminate my bell-handle, to send up your hideous name!
Mr Joseph Lebanon	Oh, Fan, I really can't! This is descendin' to a mere wrangle. Pray cut in.
Mrs Gaylustre	No, Lady Twombley, as the Season is drawing to a close, Joseph certainly does not intend to attach himself to your London establishment.
Mr Joseph Lebanon	Not for Joseph – excuse my humour.
Mrs Gaylustre	But he and I do mean to take our flight from town with the rest of the swallows. [*Pointing to a paragraph in the journal she still carries*] Look here, we saw this paragraph in the paper yesterday. Read it.

[LADY TWOMBLEY *knocks the paper to the ground*]

Lady Twombley	Insolent!
Mrs Gaylustre	Jo, pet – read it.
Mr Joseph Lebanon	Fanny, this is really most trying. [*Picking up the paper and reading*] "There are already signs of an exodus from town. Among the first of the notabilities to turn their faces northward are Sir Julian and Lady Twombley, who will spend the autumn at Drumdurris Castle as the guests of their nephew, Lord Drumdurris."
Lady Twombley	What is this to you?
Mrs Gaylustre	What's that to us!
Mr Joseph Lebanon	Fan, what's that to us! Lady Twombley, we entertain a not unreasonable desiah to spend our autumn at Drumdurris Castle.
Lady Twombley	In the kitchen?
Mr Joseph Lebanon	Oh, Fan, I really can't! You must cut in again.
Mrs Gaylustre	As the guests of Lord Drumdurris.
Lady Twombley	Never!
Mrs Gaylustre	Bill Number One falls due next month when you are at Drumdurris Castle!
Mr Joseph Lebanon	No, no! Fan, do not mix up business with friendship. You know my rule.
Mrs Gaylustre	Get us to Drumdurris and we renew!
Mr Joseph Lebanon	Oh, Fanny, how plainly you put it! Don't!
Lady Twombley	Never!

[MR MELTON *enters*]

Melton	The carriages are here, Lady Twombley.
Lady Twombley	I – I'll come.

[DRUMDURRIS *enters talking to* VALENTINE. IMOGEN, LADY EUPHEMIA, *and* BROOKE *follow; then* EGIDIA *and* ANGÈLE *with the infant*]

Mr Joseph Lebanon	[*To* LADY TWOMBLEY] Introduce me!
Lady Twombley	Never!
Mrs Gaylustre	[*To* LADY TWOMBLEY] Introduce him!

Lady Twombley	I will not!
Mr Joseph Lebanon	Lady Twombley!
	[He produces his pocketbook, opens it, and gives her a glimpse of the Bills]
Lady Twombley	The Bills! Oh!
	[SIR JULIAN *enters, intent upon his speech, the* MS *of which he carries in his hand*]
Sir Julian Twombley	*[To himself]* "I can conceive no position more agreeable to a Minister of the Crown – " *[Seeing* LEBANON] Eh?
Mrs Gaylustre	*[Whispering to* LADY TWOMBLEY] Now!
Lady Twombley	Julian, Lord Drumdurris, Brooke, let me introduce to you – Mr Lebanon.
Mrs Gaylustre	*[Triumphantly to herself]* Ah!
Mr Joseph Lebanon	*[Triumphantly to himself]* Ah! *[He grasps* SIR JULIAN'*s hand warmly]* De-lighted to find myself in your 'elegant 'ouse. Most *recherché.* *[Shaking hands with all the others]* You all know my sister, Fan. Elegant 'ouse this. Most *recherché.*
	[MRS GAYLUSTRE *runs to* SIR JULIAN *and taking a flower from her dress fastens it in his coat*]
Dowager	*[Outside]* Katherine!
	[*The* DOWAGER *enters with her arm through* MACPHAIL'*s,* LADY MACPHAIL *following*]
	I've found the truant. He had a motive.
Mr Joseph Lebanon	*[Quietly to* MRS GAYLUSTRE] Who's the Judy?
Mrs Gaylustre	*[To* LEBANON] Old Lady Drum.
Mr Joseph Lebanon	Ah! *[Turning to the* DOWAGER *and seizing her hand]* De-lighted! 'Ope to have the pleashah of meetin' you up North.
Dowager	Katherine!
	[There is a general expression of astonishment, and LADY TWOMBLEY *sinks upon the settee*]

End of the Second Act

The Third Act

Disaster

[*The scene is the inner hall at Drumdurris Castle, Perthshire,
leading on one side to the outer hall, and on the other to the
picture gallery. It is solidly and comfortably furnished, and a
fire is burning in the grate of the large oaken fireplace. It is an
afternoon in August*]

[IMOGEN *is sitting at the table reading over a letter she has
written*]

Imogen "Dear Mr White," I shall never call him Valentine again,
except in my thoughts. [*Reading*] "Dear Mr White, I
am sorry to hear that you are discontented with your
recent appointment to the Deputy-Assistant-Head-
Gamekeepership on the Drumdurris estate, and that you
consider it a sinecure fit only for a debilitated peer." Now
for it. [*Resuming*] "Permit me to take this opportunity
of informing you that I have at length consented to an
engagement between myself and Sir Colin Macphail of
Ballocheevin." Oh, how awful it looks in ink! [*Resuming*]
"As it is becoming that I should support such a position
with dignity I would prefer not encountering your dislike
to 'stuck-up people' by ever seeing you again." Oh, Val. "I
therefore suggest that you obtain a nastier appointment
than that of Deputy-Assistant-Head-Gamekeeper at
Drumdurris without delay." That will do – beautifully. [*In
tears*] Oh, Val, why have you never spoken? I know you
are poor, but I would have gone away with you and lived
cheerfully and economically in that rock if you had but
asked me. Why, why have you never asked me?

[*She sits on a footstool looking into the fire.* BROOKE, *in
shooting dress, strolls in with* LADY EUPHEMIA. *They do not see*
IMOGEN]

Brooke Twombley [*Coolly*] Well, then, Effie, I suppose I may regard our
engagement as a fixture – what? I needn't say you'll find
me an excellent husband.

Lady Euphemia Vibart Thanks awfully. But perhaps you had better mention the
subject to me again at some other time.

Brooke Twombley	Well, I shall be rather busy for the next week or two.
Lady Euphemia Vibart	Oh, quite as you please. [*Giving him her hand*] But you really are <u>too</u> impetuous.
Brooke Twombley	Not at all. [*About to kiss her*] You'll permit me, naturally?
Lady Euphemia Vibart	[*Languidly turning her cheek toward him*] Of course. Be careful of my hair — it will not be dressed again before lunch.

[*He kisses her cheek cautiously.* IMOGEN *rises without seeing them*]

[*To* BROOKE] Somebody.

[*They stroll away in opposite directions*]

Imogen	After all, as he has never been a lover, why shouldn't I see him and mention my engagement in a calm, cool, ladylike way? [*Tearing up the letter passionately*] I must see him once more — in a calm, cool, ladylike way. I'll write just a line asking him to come to me this morning.

[*As she sits to write* LADY EUPHEMIA *and* BROOKE *stroll in again and meet each other*]

Lady Euphemia Vibart	[*To* BROOKE] Good-morning.
Brooke Twombley	[*To* LADY EUPHEMIA] Good-morning.
Lady Euphemia Vibart	Why it's Imogen! Oh, let me congratulate you. [*Kissing her*] The news is <u>too</u> delightful.
Imogen	Thank you.
Brooke Twombley	Accept my congratulations also. Splendid fellow, Macphail; not one of those men who talk the top of your head off.
Imogen	[*Writing*] No, not quite. Brooke, dear, will you give Mr White a little note from me?
Brooke Twombley	Certainly. By the bye, while I think of it, you'll be glad to hear that Effie has honoured me by consenting to — er — marry me — what!
Imogen	Effie!
Lady Euphemia Vibart	How your mind does run on that subject, Brooke!
Imogen	[*Throwing her arms round* LADY EUPHEMIA's *neck*] What happy people, both of you!
Lady Euphemia Vibart	My hair!

Imogen	[*Kissing* BROOKE] A thousand congratulations, my dear, clever, old brother!
Lady Euphemia Vibart	The bother with mamma will be too wearying.
Imogen	Why a bother?
Brooke Twombley	About my pecuniary position, don't you know. You'll hardly credit it, but I haven't the least idea what pa intends to do for me.
Imogen	But it doesn't matter about that, so that you are deeply attached to each other.
Lady Euphemia Vibart	Oh, Imogen, that's <u>too</u> ridiculous!
Brooke Twombley	Quite absurd – what!
Imogen	Besides, if you want money you can work.
Brooke Twombley	Oh, it's no good everybody working. It's this stupid all-round desire to work that throws so many men out of employment. I'll look for Valentine. [IMOGEN *gives him her note*] He's sure to be about. We're going to shoot over Claigrossie Moor this morning.
	[*He goes out*]
Lady Euphemia Vibart	So you've made up your mind at last?
Imogen	No; other people have made it up for me.
Lady Euphemia Vibart	Mamma?
Imogen	Yes, Aunt Dora is the principal person who has rendered my life a burden to me.
Lady Euphemia Vibart	Oh, Imogen!
Imogen	It's true. Every hour of the livelong day Aunt Dora has goaded me on to this desirable, detestable match; even at night she has stalked into my room with a lighted candle, startling me out of my beauty sleep, to tell me she will never rest till I am Lady Macphail.
Lady Euphemia Vibart	Imogen, it's <u>too</u> kind of mamma to take this interest in you.
Imogen	Interest! It's torture. And at last she threatened that if I married anybody else she would expire in great pain and appear to me constantly, a ghost, in her night-gown. Well, you've seen Aunt Dora in her night-gown – you can guess my feelings.

Lady Euphemia Vibart And that decided you.

Imogen   I went to mamma and asked her advice.

Lady Euphemia Vibart I guess what that was.

Imogen   Mamma's expression was that she'd give the heels off her
                     best shoes to see me provided for. And so, late last night,
                     while my maid, Phipps was washing my head, I gasped
                     out a soapy sort of yes.

                     [*The* DOWAGER *enters*]

Dowager   Where is Imogen?

Lady Euphemia Vibart Here, mamma.

Dowager   [*Embracing* IMOGEN] My favourite niece! I have just learned
                     your decision over the breakfast-table. I was eating cold
                     grouse at the moment; I thought I should have choked.

Imogen   I hope you are satisfied, Aunt.

Dowager   Thoroughly. I feel now that I shall die, a great many years
                     hence, a contented woman. Effie.

Lady Euphemia Vibart Yes, mamma?

Dowager   Don't think you're neglected, child. I cannot provide for
                     everybody at once.

Lady Euphemia Vibart No, mamma.

Dowager   But having completely settled Imogen, I shall commence
                     the adjustment of your future after lunch.

                     [LADY MACPHAIL *enters*]

Lady Macphail   Ah!

Dowager   Dear Lady Macphail! What glorious news!

Lady Macphail   [*Rapturously, with her hand upraised*] Now let the worn
                     banner of the Macphail be run up on the crumbling tower
                     of Castle Ballocheevin.

Dowager   Certainly — by all means.

Lady Macphail   Now let the roar of the pipes startle the eaglets on the
                     summit of black Ben-Muchty!

Dowager   I hope such arrangements will be made.

Lady Macphail   Let the shriek of the wild birds resound on the shores of
                     Loch-na-Doich!

Dowager	[*Bringing* IMOGEN *forward*] But you haven't seen Imogen yet.
Lady Macphail	[*Embracing her*] Child! Ah, when Colin learns your answer to his suit you shall listen to such words as none but a Macphail can utter to his betrothed.
Dowager	Doesn't he know?
Lady Macphail	Not yet. He went out early to watch the sun gild the gray peak of Ben-Auchter.
	[LADY TWOMBLEY *enters, looking very troubled*]
Imogen	Mamma. [LADY MACPHAIL, *the* DOWAGER, *and* LADY EUPHEMIA *talk together*] Mamma, everybody has congratulated me. Have you nothing to say?
	[LADY TWOMBLEY *places her hand fondly on* IMOGEN'*s head*]
Lady Twombley	[*In a sepuchral voice*] Did Phipps dry your head thoroughly last night?
Imogen	Yes, mamma.
Lady Twombley	Then all's well, I suppose. [SIR JULIAN'*s flute is heard. To herself*] The first Bill — the first Bill due next week.
	[*She sits staring at the fire as* SIR JULIAN *enters, playing the flute*]
Imogen	Papa.
Sir Julian Twombley	Imogen, my dear, amidst severe official worries I must not omit to join in the general paean of rejoicing.
Imogen	Thank you, papa.
Sir Julian Twombley	Sir Colin may lack that inexhaustible flow of anecdote with which I have often been credited.
Imogen	He may, papa.
Sir Julian Twombley	But I confess I respect a man who will sit for hours without saying anything. I wish there were more like him in the House.
Dowager	Julian, let the newspapers have the details of Imogen's engagement without delay.
Imogen	Oh, no aunt! Not yet.
Dowager	Imogen, if I may use such an expression — fal-lall! Suffice it, I have a motive.
Imogen	But why the papers?

Dowager	It is our duty to our friends. Do you think if anything serious happened to me, my friends wouldn't like to hear of it without delay? Julian! [SIR JULIAN *writes*] Besides, it will be current talk at the dance tomorrow night.
Lady Macphail	The dance! Aye! Tomorrow night they shall see a Macphail lead the Strathspey with the girl who is to be his bride!
Imogen	No, indeed they won't!
Lady Macphail	What!
Imogen	I can't make myself so supremely ridiculous.
Lady Macphail	Ridiculous!
Lady Euphemia Vibart	Oh, Imogen!
Dowager	Imogen!
Lady Twombley	Imogen!
Sir Julian Twombley	My dear!

[LADY MACPHAIL *closes her eyes.* SIR JULIAN *and the* DOWAGER *take her hands*]

Sir Julian Twombley and Dowager
My dear Lady Macphail!

Lady Euphemia Vibart Here is Sir Colin!

Dowager and Sir Julian Twombley
Ah!

Lady Macphail My boy!

Lady Euphemia Vibart Why, he is with Mrs Gaylustre!

Sir Julian Twombley That woman!

Dowager That woman!

Lady Twombley That woman!

Imogen That woman!

[MACPHAIL *enters with* MRS GAYLUSTRE. *He in Highland dress, she wearing a showy costume of tweed tartan with a Scotch bonnet*]

Lady Macphail Colin, lad!

Macphail Eh, mother?

Mrs Gaylustre	Dear Sir Colin gave me his arm to the top of Ben-Auchter.
Dowager and Lady Macphail	
	To the top of Ben-Auchter!
Macphail	[*With an anxious glance at* MRS GAYLUSTRE] Just to see the sun rise.
Dowager	[*Quietly to* SIR JULIAN] Julian, that's scandalous!
Lady Macphail	I thought you always witnessed the sun rise alone, Colin.
Macphail	As a rule, mother.
Dowager	[*To herself*] That woman has a motive.
Lady Macphail	[*Pointing to* IMOGEN] My son, look – here is Imogen.
Macphail	[*To* IMOGEN] Good-morning.
Lady Macphail	Colin, lad, don't you guess?
Macphail	No, mother.
Lady Macphail	[*Rapturously*] Now let the worn banner of the Macphail be run up on the crumbling tower of Castle Ballocheevin!
Macphail	[*Vacantly*] For what reason, mother?
Lady Macphail	Now let the shriek of the wild birds sound on the shores of Loch-na-Doich!
Macphail	Why?
Lady Macphail	[*Embracing* MACPHAIL] Imogen is to be your bride.
Macphail	[*Blankly*] Oh!
	[SIR JULIAN, *the* DOWAGER *and* LADY EUPHEMIA *congratulate him*]
Sir Julian Twombley	Most gratified!
Dowager	I have a mother's yearnings towards you.
Lady Euphemia Vibart	We are <u>too</u> rejoiced.
Mrs Gaylustre	[*To herself*] They've hooked him!
Lady Macphail	[*Bringing* MACPHAIL *down*] Hush! Speak to her, Colin, lad. Let her hear how a Macphail greets the woman of his choice.
	[LADY MACPHAIL *joins* SIR JULIAN, *the* DOWAGER *and* LADY EUPHEMIA, *while they all watch* MACPHAIL *as he approaches* IMOGEN]
	Listen!

Macphail	[*To* IMOGEN] Er — I'm very much obliged to ye.
Lady Macphail	Bravely spoken!
Dowager	A grand nature!
Imogen	Thank you, Sir Colin.
	[*She joins the others*]
Mrs Gaylustre	[*To* MACPHAIL, *seizing his hand*] May your life be very, very blissful!
Macphail	[*Uneasily, withdrawing his hand*] Mother's looking.
	[*He joins the rest*]
Mrs Gaylustre	[*To herself*] They've hooked my Scotch salmon; but they haven't landed him yet! [*Intercepting* LADY TWOMBLEY *as she advances towards the group*] Kate!
Lady Twombley	Reptile!
Mrs Gaylustre	I'm not at all satisfied with the way things are going on here.
Lady Twombley	Aren't you? I think things are beautifully smooth.
Mrs Gaylustre	I'm pretty comfortable at Drumdurris myself, thank you; but I'm getting extremely anxious about Joseph.
Lady Twombley	So am I.
Mrs Gaylustre	I'm afraid Joseph isn't enjoying his little holiday at all. Did you observe him at dinner last night?
Lady Twombley	Who could help it? The man eats enough for six.
Mrs Gaylustre	He's obliged to, his holiday being so brief. But these fine folks treat him as contemptuously as if he were a snail in a cabbage.
Lady Twombley	Then why does he talk with the leg of a grouse sticking out of the side of his mouth? Why does he drink people's health across the table and call men-servants "old chaps?"
Mrs Gaylustre	Dear Jo! There's nothing classy about him.
	[DRUMDURRIS, *in shooting dress, enters, carrying a light wooden box*]
Lady Twombley	Why does he swallow his knife and build pyramids with his bread; and tell long stories with no meaning at all or else with two?

Mrs Gaylustre	Well, you must take Jo as Heaven made him. So you'd better make things smooth for him with Lord Drumdurris. If not —
Lady Twombley	If not?
Mrs Gaylustre	If not, Jo might, after all, decline to renew.
Lady Twombley	Oh!
Mrs Gaylustre	And then there would be the devil to pay, wouldn't there?
Lady Twombley	As far as I can see there are two devils to pay already.
Mrs Gaylustre	Ha, ha! Here's Drumdurris. Remember.
	[*After talking to the others,* DRUMDURRIS *approaches* LADY TWOMBLEY, *bowing stiffly to* MRS GAYLUSTRE, *who shakes her fist behind his back.* LADY TWOMBLEY *gives a small nervous shriek*]
Earl of Drumdurris	Aunt?
Lady Twombley	[*With her hand to her heart*] Spasms.
Mrs Gaylustre	[*Smiling sweetly at* DRUMDURRIS] Delightful morning.
	[*She takes up a newspaper.* SIR JULIAN *and* LADY EUPHEMIA *stroll out*]
Lady Twombley	[*To* DRUMDURRIS] Keith, dear, I want to say a word to you about — dear Mr Lebanon.
Earl of Drumdurris	Ah! Aunt!
Lady Twombley	Have patience, Keith!
Earl of Drumdurris	Patience!
Lady Twombley	When I begged you to entertain him at Drumdurris I didn't deceive you. I distinctly told you he was one of nature's noblemen.
Earl of Drumdurris	I would do much to please you, Aunt Kate, but this individual and his sister —
Lady Twombley	You must follow the democratic tendencies of the age, Keith. The peer must go hand in hand with the pig.
Earl of Drumdurris	Yes, but let it be the companionable, clubable pig. Oh, I have just left him at the breakfast-table.
Lady Twombley	Is he making a tolerable breakfast this morning?
Earl of Drumdurris	He seems to be making every breakfast in Great Britain.
Lady Twombley	I see him at it.

Earl of Drumdurris	He consumes enough coffee to put a fire out.
Lady Twombley	Yes; and he swoops down on a cold bird like a vulture.
Earl of Drumdurris	It's hideous to see him hurl himself at an omelette.
Lady Twombley	I know; and with eggs he's a conjuror. What's he engaged on now?
Earl of Drumdurris	When I left him he was an unrecognizable mass of marmalade. He must go!
Lady Twombley	Don't disregard the sacred laws of hospitality!
Earl of Drumdurris	I must. At another time I might endure him, but now when I am utterly crushed by my own agonizing trouble – Hark!
Lady Twombley	What's the matter?
Earl of Drumdurris	My son.

[ANGÈLE *appears with the infant*]

Angèle	[*Mysteriously*] Is it alright, milord?
Earl of Drumdurris	Hush! [*To* LADY TWOMBLEY] Is Egidia there?

[SIR JULIAN *and* LADY EUPHEMIA *re-enter*]

Lady Twombley	No.

[LADY TWOMBLEY *joins* SIR JULIAN *and* LADY EUPHEMIA]

Earl of Drumdurris	[*To* ANGÈLE] All right. [*Fondly to the infant*] My soldier boy! [ANGÈLE *advances to* DRUMDURRIS. *He produces a small toy gun and a little drum from a box he carries and hands them to* ANGÈLE] Don't let Lady Drumdurris discover these.
Angèle	No.
Earl of Drumdurris	Above all, let the drum be muffled.
Angèle	Yees, milord.

[EGIDIA *enters*]

Earl of Drumdurris	I expect some small cannon by the evening post. Go.

[EGIDIA *comes between* ANGÈLE *and* DRUMDURRIS, *the* DOWAGER *following*]

	Ah!
Angèle	Oh, miladi!
Egidia	I am right, then.

[*She takes the toys from* ANGÈLE *and points to the door.* ANGÈLE *withdraws with the infant*]

Dowager Keith – Egidia! Don't disagree here!

Egidia [*To* DRUMDURRIS] I was loth to credit you with such treachery.

Dowager Name some convenient hour to disagree this afternoon. I will willingly be present.

Egidia I have long suspected this conspiracy to anticipate my son's mature judgement. Keith, there is a gulf between us which can never be bridged over.

[EGIDIA *joins the others*]

Earl of Drumdurris Mother, my life is wasted.

[VALENTINE, *roughly dressed in cords and gaiters, enters, followed by* BROOKE]

Valentine White Are you ready, Lord Drumdurris?

Earl of Drumdurris We are waiting, I presume, for Mr Lebanon.

Brooke Twombley I'll go and stir him up. Ugh! What!

[BROOKE *goes out*]

Earl of Drumdurris You'll not join us, Sir Julian?

Sir Julian Twombley I daren't. Melton has arrived from town with a mass of papers for my signature. [*Quietly to* DRUMDURRIS] The Rajputana Canal Question is wearing me out.

Valentine White [*Whispering to* IMOGEN] I have your note. I'll return in a few minutes.

Mr Joseph Lebanon [*Outside*] Shootin', my dear sir! When I was in the South 'Ampstead Artillery I could have shown you what shootin' was.

Mrs Gaylustre There's Jo.

[*She goes out to meet* LEBANON]

All [*With various expressions of disgust*] Ugh! That man!

[*All gather into groups, as* LEBANON, *looking very ridiculous in Highland costume, enters, followed by* BROOKE]

Mr Joseph Lebanon [*Slapping* MACPHAIL *on the back*] Mac, dear old boy, 'aven't seen you this morning. [MACPHAIL *turns away distrustfully*] Lady Mac, I 'ear delightful whispers.

Lady Macphail	Sir?
Mr Joseph Lebanon	An 'approaching 'appy event. We're like the doves – we're pairin' off, hey; we're pairin' off?

[LADY MACPHAIL *stares at him and turns away. He wipes his forehead anxiously*]

It's a little difficult to keep up a long conversation with 'em. They're not what I should term Rattlers. [*Eyeing* EGIDIA] The fair 'ostess. Ahem! We missed you at the breakfast table, Lady Drum. Can't congratulate you on your peck – excuse my humour.

[EGIDIA *stares at him and joins* LADY MACPHAIL]

[*To himself*] They're a chatty lot; I must say they're a chatty lot. I wish Fanny would stick by me and cut in occasionally. There's Lady T. She can't ride the 'igh 'orse, at any rate. Lady T.

Lady Twombley	Mr Lebanon?
Mr Joseph Lebanon	You didn't honour me with my game of crib last night.
Lady Twombley	I – I had a headache.
Mr Joseph Lebanon	Never 'ad a 'eadache in my life – don't know 'ow it's spelt.
Lady Twombley	It's spelt with an H.
Mr Joseph Lebanon	[*To* LADY EUPHEMIA, *offering her flowers from his coat*] Lady, Effie, my floral offering.

[LADY EUPHEMIA *catches up her skirts and sweeps past him*]

[*To himself*] Chatty, hey? Chatty? [*He comes face to face with the* DOWAGER, *who glares at him*] Hah! H'm! [*Offering her the flowers*] I – ah – had these picked for you, by Jove, I did. A present from Joseph.

Dowager	What, sir!
Mr Joseph Lebanon	[*Replacing the flowers in his coat*] Excuse my humour. [*Wiping his brow again*] Chatty! I do wish Fan would cut in and help me. [*Slaps* SIR JULIAN *on the shoulder*] Twombley, old fellow.
Sir Julian Twombley	Sir!
Mr Joseph Lebanon	Not comin' out with us today, hey!
Sir Julian Twombley	No.

Mr Joseph Lebanon	Gettin' past it, I suppose?
Sir Julian Twombley	I am kept indoors by pressure of work, Mr Lebanon.
Mr Joseph Lebanon	Oh, of course, the Rajputana Canal Question, hey? I'm a big shareholder in the Rajputana Railway, yer know. I say, tell me —
Sir Julian Twombley	I cannot discuss official matters with you.
	[SIR JULIAN *turns from him*]
Mr Joseph Lebanon	[*To himself as he sits down*] Chatty! Chatty! I know what this'll end in. It'll end in my standin' on my dignity. Where's Fanny? [*Addressing the others*] Talkin' about shootin', I'll you an amusin' little story.
Sir Julian Twombley	[*To* LADY TWOMBLEY *and others sotto voce*] No, no!
Mr Joseph Lebanon	It's all about myself.
Brooke Twombley	[*Whispering to the others*] Good-bye. We're off.
	[*There is general movement, the ladies and* SIR JULIAN *saying good-bye to the shooters, unnoticed by* LEBANON, *who has his back to them*]
Mr Joseph Lebanon	I was spendin' a day or two down in Essex with my old friend, Captain Bolter, South 'Ampstead Artillery. Dear old Tom — great favourite with the gals. Excuse my humour.

Lady Twombley, Imogen, Lady Euphemia Vibart, Sir Julian Twombley, Lady Macphail and the Dowager

    [*Quietly to the shooters*] Good-bye.

Mr Joseph Lebanon	It was wild-fowl Tom and I were after. We were lyin' in a ditch waitin' for the ducks to drift in with the tide.

    [*As* LEBANON *continues his story all the others gradually and quietly disperse*]

    I counted fifty-seven birds through my glass. So said I to Tom, "Tom, I'm in dooced good form, my boy." "Devil you are!" said Tom. "And I lay you a pony to a penny that fifteen of those birds fall to my gun." "Done!" said Tom. [*He is now alone in the room*] Well, to make a short story a long one — excuse my humour — Tom sneezed. Up I got. So did the ducks. And then what the dooce d'ye think 'appened? I say, what the dooce d'ye think — [*Discovering that he is alone*] Well, I'm — Chatty, ain't they? Chatty!

Mrs Gaylustre	Jo! Why aren't you with the shooters?
Mr Joseph Lebanon	Why! They hooked it while I was tellin' 'em the tale of Tom Bolter and the ducks.
Mrs Gaylustre	Never mind, my pet.
Mr Joseph Lebanon	It's rude – that's what it is – it's dooced rude.
Mrs Gaylustre	Come along, we'll walk on to the moor.
Mr Joseph Lebanon	What, are you going too, Fan?
Mrs Gaylustre	Yes, dear. Your poor Fanny has a little bit of fun on.
Mr Joseph Lebanon	Oh, Fan, if I only 'ad your confidence, your push. But the rudeness of these people is gettin' on my nerves.
Mrs Gaylustre	Why, Joseph!
Mr Joseph Lebanon	I feel a little 'urt, Fan – a little 'urt.
	[VALENTINE *enters*]
Valentine White	Mr Lebanon!
Mr Joseph Lebanon	Hi! Where are they?
Valentine White	Just starting in the drag. Be quick.
Mr Joseph Lebanon	[*To* MRS GAYLUSTRE] Come on! They shall hear about Tom Bolter and the ducks before I've done with 'em. Come on!
	[MRS GAYLUSTRE *and* LEBANON *hurry out*]
	[*Outside*] Hi! Hi!
Valentine White	That fellow was born to hail an omnibus.
	[IMOGEN *appears*]
Imogen	[*Not seeing* VALENTINE] Will he be long? [*She encounters him*] Oh! You are not neglecting your duties, I hope, Valentine?
Valentine White	I shall follow the others in the cart. Your note was marked "urgent".
Imogen	Was it?
Valentine White	[*Showing her letter*] "Urgent."
Imogen	What a thoughtless habit it is to mark all one's letters "urgent." All I wanted to say to you is this – but it isn't urgent.

Valentine White	No, no – I understand that.
Imogen	I merely had a foolish desire to be the first to acquaint you of my – undeserved happiness.
Valentine White	What happiness don't you deserve?
Imogen	The happiness of becoming Lady Colin Macphail, Valentine.
Valentine White	Oh. Is that – all?
Imogen	That's all – just at present.
Valentine White	Hah! You'll be a fine lady now, past recovery.
Imogen	I shall endeavour to adequately fill the station of life to which fate has called me.
Valentine White	All that sweet simplicity of yours in London was purely an assumption, I suppose?
Imogen	Things are – what they appear.
Valentine White	But you have your heart's desire at last, I presume?
Imogen	I – I presume I have.
Valentine White	[*Burying his head in his hands*] Oh!
Imogen	What are you going to do next?
Valentine White	Japan.
Imogen	Nice part of Japan?
Valentine White	The murderous districts.
Imogen	Oh! Then you don't propose to – return alive?
Valentine White	Not according to my present arrangements.
Imogen	You – you had better follow the shooters to Claigrossie now.
Valentine White	Certainly.
Imogen	I am glad to have had this gossip over our prospects. We – we both seem to be doing well. Good-morning.
	[*She offers her hand, which he takes ungraciously*]
Valentine White	Good-morning.
Imogen	You haven't congratulated me yet – in the usual way.
Valentine White	Will you be happy with – him?

Imogen	I think – partially.
Valentine White	But you're not going to partially marry Sir Colin. How dare you do this?
Imogen	He was the first to ask me, Val.
Valentine White	The first to ask you! You don't mean to suggest that any other man would have done!
Imogen	No – not <u>any</u> other.
Valentine White	<u>Some</u> other?
Imogen	It's too late now – but yes.
Valentine White	A poor man?
Imogen	Val!
Valentine White	Would <u>I</u> have stood the remotest chance?
Imogen	It's too late now.
Valentine White	Would I? Would I?
Imogen	No. Nor any other nineteenth century savage.
Valentine White	Savage!
Imogen	Mr White, it is very much too late now; but why, when you returned to England, didn't you wear uncomfortable clothes like other gentlemen, and a very high collar, and varnished boots, like other gentlemen?
Valentine White	Why? Because I cannot be false to my principles.
Imogen	People say that principles which deal too much with the outside of things are nothing but affectation.
Valentine White	Imogen!
Imogen	If a man has a good heart he should have a good hat.
Valentine White	Imogen – Jenny! If I had ever come to you – in a good hat –
Imogen	If you had, then when mamma urged me to marry perhaps she would not have blamed me for –
Valentine White	For what?
Imogen	For, liking some pleasant-looking gentleman who laughed at harmless follies instead of scolding them.
Valentine White	And now?

Imogen	Now! Now – it is too late.
	[*She falls into his arms; he embraces her*]
Mr Joseph Lebanon	[*Outside*] Hi! Hi! Come here! Hi!
Imogen	Ah!
	[*She breaks from* VALENTINE *and runs out as* LEBANON *enters, very pale and upset*]
Mr Joseph Lebanon	[*Clinging to* VALENTINE] Old fellow!
Valentine White	What's the matter with you?
Mr Joseph Lebanon	Gurrrh! You, you're wanted!
	[LADY TWOMBLEY *enters*]
Lady Twombley	Good gracious!
Valentine White	Something has happened, I'm afraid.
	[VALENTINE *goes out*]
Lady Twombley	[*To* LEBANON] You're ill!
Mr Joseph Lebanon	I'm upset.
Lady Twombley	Too much breakfast!
Mr Joseph Lebanon	No. I – I've peppered Macphail.
Lady Twombley	Peppered him! Can't you take your mind off eating?
Mr Joseph Lebanon	You don't understand. I was in the wagonette, telling 'em the story of Tom Bolter and these beastly ducks. I got 'old of a beastly gun and just as I was demonstrating how I shot the fifteen beastly birds . . .
Lady Twombley	It went off!
Mr Joseph Lebanon	Well! Don't make such a fuss about it!
Lady Twombley	Ah! And it was pointed at Sir Colin!
Mr Joseph Lebanon	Pointed at him! No! His legs were stuck right in the way.
Lady Twombley	Heavens!
Mr Joseph Lebanon	Be quiet! Make light of it – make light of it, like I do!
Lady Twombley	Now, now I hope you're content!
Mr Joseph Lebanon	No, I'm not. I wouldn't have had this 'appen for 'alf a sovereign. This 'Ighland 'oliday of mine is gettin' on my nerves.

Lady Twombley	Your nerves!
Mr Joseph Lebanon	Yes, Lady T. Imagine what it must mean to a shy man to spend a rollickin' August with a lot of people whose chief occupation is staring at the tips of their own aquiline noses.
Lady Twombley	[*Hysterically*] Ha, ha, ha!
Mr Joseph Lebanon	Imagine what it must be to a shy man to find himself always leading the conversation, instead of following it with a sparkling comment or two, as I'm in the 'abit of doin' in my own circle. Think of me starting every topic and arguing on it till my throat's sore, making every joke and roaring at it till I get blood to the head. Sometimes when I'm in the middle of a long story and not a soul listening I feel so lonely I – I could almost cry.
Lady Twombley	Then out of your own sufferings why can't you find some compassion for mine?
Mr Joseph Lebanon	It's pathetic – that's what my position is – it's dooced pathetic.
Lady Twombley	In mercy's name why don't you retire quietly to your room and pack?
Mr Joseph Lebanon	What! Throw up the sponge?
Lady Twombley	You needn't throw up your sponge – <u>pack</u> your sponge.
Mr Joseph Lebanon	I understand, Lady T – hook it!
Lady Twombley	"Hook it" is a harsh way of putting it. Bring your visit to a close. Think of what you are losing here! Think of Margate, where I feel you must have many dear friends!
Mr Joseph Lebanon	I – I've half a mind to.
Lady Twombley	Ha! Bless you, Mr Lebanon, bless you! I'll fetch you a Bradshaw.
Mr Joseph Lebanon	Stop! I forgot the hop.
Lady Twombley	The hop?
Mr Joseph Lebanon	There's a ball here tomorrow night.
Lady Twombley	For heaven's sake, don't wait for the hop.
Mr Joseph Lebanon	I had half-a-dozen lessons in the Scotch Reel before I left town.

Lady Twombley	And you would risk the Reel on half-a-dozen lessons! Madman!
Mr Joseph Lebanon	Half-a-dozen lessons at store prices. Dash it all, you wouldn't 'ave me waste 'em!
Lady Twombley	Hopeless!

[SIR JULIAN *enters unobserved by* LEBANON *or* LADY TWOMBLEY]

Mr Joseph Lebanon	Look ' ere, Lady T! I'm sorry to disappoint a lady, but it aint Mr Joseph Lebanon's principle to do something for nothing.
Lady Twombley	No. If you lent a lady your arm you'd do it at interest.
Mr Joseph Lebanon	I'm not alludin' to our pleasant financial relationship, Lady T. What I infer is that if after the forthcoming hop I drag myself away from my sorrowin' friends at Drumdurris I expect a – ah – a solatium.

[SIR JULIAN *remains watching and listening*]

Lady Twombley	A what?
Mr Joseph Lebanon	Lady T, my pride has been wounded in this 'ouse – my self-respect has been 'urt.
Lady Twombley	Ha, ha, ha! Pardon me, I'm hysterical.
Mr Joseph Lebanon	If you could 'eal my feelings by rendering me a little service –
Lady Twombley	To be rid of you?
Mr Joseph Lebanon	Oh, Lady T, 'ow plainly you put it! Well, yes.
Lady Twombley	Try me.

[SIR JULIAN *disappears suddenly*]

Mr Joseph Lebanon	'Ush! Thought I 'eard somebody. Lady T, you are aware that Mr Joseph Lebanon's position in the financial world is an eminent one.
Lady Twombley	I wasn't aware of it.
Mr Joseph Lebanon	Take it from me, Lady T, take it from me. But that distinguished position might be advanced by the success of some delicate little financial operations which I'm on the brink of, Lady Twomley, on the brink of. Lady T, if I could know twenty-four hours in advance of the prying newspapers the decision of the Government on

	the Rajputana Canal Question it would go far to 'eal the wound my self-respect has received in this *recherché* 'Ighland 'ome. You follow me, Lady T?
Lady Twombley	I suppose you mean that when the decision of the Government is known in the City something or other will go up and something or other will go down on the Stock Exchange? Is that it?
Mr Joseph Lebanon	That's it, Lady T, that's it! And some fellers will make fortunes! Oh, Lady T!
Lady Twombley	But why do you bother a poor woman with a headache –
Mr Joseph Lebanon	Because without the gentle guidance of tender-hearted women I can't find out whether the Government is going to grant the concession for the cutting of the Rajputana Canal. Oh, Lady Twombley, let me 'ave five minutes alone with Sir Julian's papers in Sir Julian's room.
Lady Twombley	Mr Lebanon!
Mr Joseph Lebanon	Two minutes! A stroll round. I'll go in with a duster and tidy up.
Lady Twombley	Oh!
Mr Joseph Lebanon	Or give me a glimpse of some of the documents Mr Melton brought with him in that box yesterday.
Lady Twombley	I want some fresh air!
Mr Joseph Lebanon	Wait! If you'll do this for me I'll clear out of Drumdurris with Fanny on Thursday morning.
Lady Twombley	Ah, no!
Mr Joseph Lebanon	And I'll hand you back your acceptances – every one of 'em – I will – on my word of honour as a gentleman!
	[*She seizes him by the throat and shakes him violently*]
Lady Twombley	How dare you! How dare you tempt me!
Mr Joseph Lebanon	[*Arranging his hair and moustache with his pocket comb and mirror*] Oh, ladies are trying in business – they are dooced trying.
Lady Twombley	You – you wretch! Do you think I haven't endured enough for the past three months without this? Oh, pa, what will you say to your Kitty when you know the disgrace she's brought on you! Oh, my chicks, my chicks, my blessed chicks!

Mr Joseph Lebanon	Lady Twombley, my pride has been wounded, my self-respect has been 'urt in this *recherché* 'Ighland 'ome for, I 'ope, the last time. I shall retire from the hop early tomorrow night and hook it – bring my visit to a close – on Thursday morning.
Lady Twombley	Thank you.
Mr Joseph Lebanon	Next week the first bit of paper bearin' the honoured name of woman falls doo.
Lady Twombley	Oh!
Mr Joseph Lebanon	I repeat the word, d-u-e, doo.
Lady Twombley	Mr Lebanon!
Mr Joseph Lebanon	Our interview has been a distressin' one, Lady Twombley. It is over.
Lady Twombley	Mr Lebanon! Mr Lebanon! [*He turns his chair from her. To herself*] It's all up with me. I – I'll go and find pa, and tell him. There's no help for it – I'll tell him. Mr Lebanon! For the last time – have compassion on a poor fool of a woman! [*He turns away*] Oh! I'll go to pa's room and – tell him.
	[*She goes out*]
Mr Joseph Lebanon	That's one way to the old gentleman's room. [*He opens the door and listens*] Ah! What's the latest quotation for lovely woman's weakness?
	[VALENTINE *enters with* MRS GAYLUSTRE *and* MACPHAIL, *who looks very scared, has a handkerchief bound round his knee, and leans on* MRS GAYLUSTRE*'s arm. She supports him to a chair*]
Mrs Gaylustre	[*To Sir Colin*] Lean on your poor broken-hearted friend.
Mr Joseph Lebanon	[*To himself*] Oh, the dooce!
Valentine White	I'll find Lady Macphail.
	[*He goes out*]
Mrs Gaylustre	[*Whispering to* LEBANON] Get out of sight!
Mr Joseph Lebanon	[*Quietly to her*] Can't. I must wait here – I've got an important little affair on.
Mrs Gaylustre	So have I. Leave us!
Mr Joseph Lebanon	Oh, my goodness, how selfish you are, Fanny!

Mrs Gaylustre	Selfish! You'll ruin my prospects in life! Brute!
Mr Joseph Lebanon	Vixen!
Mrs Gaylustre	Bah!
Mr Joseph Lebanon	Bah!

[LEBANON *goes out.* MRS GAYLUSTRE *throws herself on her knees beside* MACPHAIL]

Mrs Gaylustre	How do you feel now?
Macphail	Well, it's tingling.
Mrs Gaylustre	Tingling! You bear it like a hero.
Macphail	I appreciate the compliment, but I'm thinking I'm only a bit singed.
Mrs Gaylustre	Ah, but why, why do you indulge in these reckless sports?
Macphail	I was merely sitting in the drag looking at the sky.
Mrs Gaylustre	Sitting in the drag looking at the sky! How foolhardy!
Macphail	Whereupon your brother, without a word of warning, blazed away at my knee.
Mrs Gaylustre	Ah! don't describe it! Suppose you had had your head on your knee!
Lady Macphail	[*Outside*] Take me to Colin!
Macphail	My mother!
Mrs Gaylustre	[*To herself*] Drat your mother.

[*She stands with her handkerchief to her eyes.* LADY MACPHAIL *enters with* EGIDIA, *the* DOWAGER, LADY EUPHEMIA, *and* VALENTINE]

Egidia	Sir Colin!
Dowager	[*Sitting at the writing-table*] I'll telegraph to Sir George McHarness, the surgeon.
Lady Macphail	Now let the wail of lament waken the echoes of black Ben-Muchty!
Macphail	[*Rising from the chair*] It's not at all necessary, mother.
Egidia	He can stand!
Dowager	[*Writing*] "Bring – chloroform – and knives."
Lady Macphail	Ah, Colin, lad, why did we ever quit the gray shores of Loch-na-Doich?

Macphail	I'll go upstairs and bathe my knee, mother.
	[LADY MACPHAIL *leads him*]
Egidia	He can walk!
Lady Macphail	Madam, a Macphail can always walk under any circumstances.
Dowager	[*Reading the telegram she has written*] "If – in – doubt – amputate."
	[LADY MACPHAIL, MACPHAIL, VALENTINE, LADY EUPHEMIA, EGIDIA *and the* DOWAGER *go out*]
Mrs Gaylustre	[*Weeping till the others are out of sight*] Joseph will die of remorse! [*Calling*] The coast is clear, Joseph. Jo!
	[*As she goes out* LADY TWOMBLEY *enters in great agitation, clutching an important-looking document*]
Lady Twombley	Kitty, what have you done! Kitty, what have you done!
	[LEBANON *enters*]
Mr Joseph Lebanon	Lady T. Thought so! [*Seeing the paper*] Oh, my goodness, what has she got there?
Lady Twombley	I must – I must find Julian! Oh!
Mr Joseph Lebanon	[*Snatching the paper*] Excuse me!
Lady Twombley	Ah! Give me back that paper!
Mr Joseph Lebanon	Lady T, oh, Lady T!
Lady Twombley	[*Following him round the table*] Give me back that paper! Dear, sweet, Mr Lebanon!
Lady Twombley	[*Reading the paper*] Ha!
Lady Twombley	Ah! Don't read it!
Mr Joseph Lebanon	My friend Sir Julian's own writing! The Rajputana Canal is a blessed fact! Lady Twombley, I forget my wounded pride, I forgive the blow to my self-respect. You have won a place in Jo Lebanon's heart.
Lady Twombley	Give me back that paper and forget it!
Mr Joseph Lebanon	[*Returning the paper*] Give it you back? Delighted. Forget it? Oh, Lady T, Lady T.
Lady Twombley	Devil!

Mr Joseph Lebanon	Lady Twombley, Joseph Lebanon is, above all things, a man of honour. [*Handing Bills to* LADY TWOMBLEY] Lovely woman's Acceptances.
Lady Twombley	I won't take them. I won't buy them back at such a price.
Mr Joseph Lebanon	Natural delicacy. [*Laying the Bills on the table*] You can pick 'em up when I'm gone.
Lady Twombley	Oh, what a wicked woman I am!
Mr Joseph Lebanon	I can get out of these beastly clothes, drive to Strachlachan Junction, and wire to town before feedin' time. The City is on the eve of a financial earthquake! Joseph's name will be a 'ouse'old word from Mile End to Kensington! Lady Twombley, we meet at the hop tomorrow night for the last time – in Society. [*Boisterously*] Whoop! Dash Society! [*He performs a few steps of a Highland dance*] Excuse my humour.
	[*He goes out*]
Lady Twombley	The Bills! The Bills! They mustn't lie there.
	[*As she goes to the table* SIR JULIAN, *looking very white and dishevelled, enters, and, standing opposite to her, takes up the Bills and presents them to her*]
	Pa!
Sir Julian Twombley	Lady Twombley!
Lady Twombley	Oh, my gracious!
	[*She drops on her hands and knees at* SIR JULIAN'*s feet*]
	You've found me out, pa! You've found me out!
Sir Julian Twombley	I have found you out.
Lady Twombley	How did you manage it?
Sir Julian Twombley	By degrading myself to the position of an eavesdropper.
Lady Twombley	That's pretty mean, pa – ain't it?
	[*Seeing that he is examining the Bills she puts up her hands and seizes them*]
	Ah! Don't tot them up! Don't tot them up!
Sir Julian Twombley	Katherine, when I first saw you, three-and-twenty years ago, you were standing over a tub in the tiled yard of your father's farm wringing out your little sister's pinafores.

Lady Twombley	[*Weeping*] Oh-h-h!
Sir Julian Twombley	Could I have looked forward I should have known that you would one day wring my feelings as you do now.
Lady Twombley	Pa, I've fallen into the hands of the unscrupulous.
Sir Julian Twombley	Woman!
Lady Twombley	Oh, don't call me that, pa!
Sir Julian Twombley	The unscrupulous! You have lost the right to ever again use that serviceable word.
Lady Twombley	What do you mean?
Sir Julian Twombley	How do you come by those Bills?
Lady Twombley	Julian, you know! [*Going toward him on her knees frantically*] Ah, don't stare like that! [*Putting her arms round him*] Husband! Dear husband, you are glaring like an idiot! Listen! [*She shakes him violently*] Listen! When that reptile tempted me I ran upstairs intending to tell you all. I did. Oh, pa, don't stare at nothing! I knocked at your door; there was a drumming in my ears, and I fancied your voice answered me telling me to enter. Oh, try winking, pa, try winking! Your room was empty – left unguarded, the door unlocked. I entered. Wink, pa; for mercy's sake, wink! I sank into a chair to wait for your coming, [*Taking the written paper from her pocket*] and there, on your table, right before my eyes, I saw this thing like a white ghost.
Sir Julian Twombley	A memorandum in my writing that the concession for the Rajuputana Canal is to be granted.
Lady Twombley	Yes, yes. I tried to forget it was there. But the chairs and tables seemed to dance before me and every object in the room had a voice crying out "Kitty, you silly woman, get back your Bills from that demon who is plaguing you!" I put my fingers in my ears and then the voices were shut up in my brain, and still they shrieked, "Kitty, get back your Bills! Get back your Bills!" I snatched up this paper and ran from the room. Even then if I had met you, Julian, I should have been safe; but whenever Old Nick wants to play the deuce with a married lady he begins by taking her husband for a stroll, and so I fell into Lebanon's clutches – and I – I – I'm done for!
	[*She sinks into a chair*]

Sir Julian Twombley	Katherine, those Bills must be returned to the creature, Lebanon.
Lady Twombley	Yes. And – and – pa, dear, you'll never speak kindly to me after this, will you?
Sir Julian Twombley	I trust I shall be invariably polite to you, Katherine.
Lady Twombley	Oh-h-h! We shall be whitewashed in the Bankruptcy Court eventually, I suppose?
Sir Julian Twombley	All in good time, Katherine.
Lady Twombley	And then – what then?
Sir Julian Twombley	Then we must hope for a cottage, and a small garden where we can grow our own vegetables and learn wisdom.
Lady Twombley	Our – own – vegetables. And years hence, pa, sometimes when I am sitting over my knitting, you'll forget the past, and play your flute again, and be happy?
Sir Julian Twombley	Katherine! [*He takes his flute from his pocket and breaks it into pieces across his knee*] Never, never again, Katherine. [*As he is leaving her*] One pang of remorse I can spare you, Katherine.
Lady Twombley	Don't!
Sir Julian Twombley	You believe you have betrayed a solemn secret of the Government to that unprincipled money-lender.
Lady Twombley	Of course.
Sir Julian Twombley	That you have <u>not</u> done.
Lady Twombley	Pa!
Sir Julian Twombley	No, Katherine. Overhearing his shameful proposition, and fearing your weakness, I had time to hasten to my room, conceal all important papers, and scribble the memorandum you abstracted.
Lady Twombley	Why, then –
Sir Julian Twombley	That writing records the exact reverse of the truth.
Lady Twombley	And – and Joseph?
Sir Julian Twombley	In the language of the vulgar – Mr Lebanon is sold.

[*He goes out*]

Lady Twombley	Julian! Ah! [*Staring at the paper*] The exact reverse of the truth! Then the Rajputana Canal — Julian, why should you be first blackened and then whitewashed because of your vagabond wife? A cottage — our own vegetables! Never! Why shouldn't I have <u>my</u> delicate little financial operations in the City? Oh, my gracious!

[DRUMDURRIS *and* BROOKE *enter*]

Brooke Twombley	Hullo, Mater — what!
Lady Twombley	Brooke! Keith! You boys must drive me over to Strachlachan Junction. I must telegraph to London backwards and forwards all day. Keith, put me into communication with your Stockbroker in town!
Earl of Drumdurris	Aunt!
Lady Twombley	Silence! I'm on the brink of some delicate little financial operations! [*To* BROOKE] Get out the cart!
Brooke Twombley	The drag's outside.
Lady Twombley	Come on!

[LEBANON *enters hastily*]

Mr Joseph Lebanon	Hi, Drumdurris! Let me 'ave a carriage to go to Strachlachan Junction. I want to wire to town.
Lady Twombley	Do you? So do we. We'll give you a lift. Come on!

[*They all hurry out*]

End of the Third Act

The Fourth Act

Dancing

[*The scene is still the inner hall of Drumdurris Castle, now brilliantly lighted and florally decorated, the evening after the events of the previous act*]

[*Waltz-music is heard, then a slight scream, and* LEBANON *in full Highland costume, enters hastily*]

Mr Joseph Lebanon I wouldn't 'ave 'ad it 'appen for 'alf a sovereign. .

[THE MUNKITTRICK, *a fiery old gentleman in Highland dress, enters*]

The Munkittrick Sir, I am most indignant!

Mr Joseph Lebanon I've explained. I felt myself goin' and I caught at what came nearest.

The Munkittrick My daughter came nearest.

Mr Joseph Lebanon I know. Don't make such a fuss about it! Do remember we're at a ball!

The Munkittrick Miss Munkittrick is torn to ribbons.

Mr Joseph Lebanon All right. Make light of it — make light of it, like I do.

The Munkittrick Ah-h-h!

[DRUMDURRIS, *in Highland dress, enters with* MISS MUNKITTRICK, *who is much discomposed, and* EGIDIA *who is soothing her*]

Earl of Drumdurris [*To* MUNKITTRICK] My dear sir!

Miss Munkittrick Papa!

Egidia Oh, Flora, Flora!

The Munkittrick Lord Drumdurris!

Mr Joseph Lebanon Let it blow over. We're all forgettin' we're at a ball.

The Munkittrick Miss Munkittrick has been rolled upon the floor.

Mr Joseph Lebanon She was passin' at the time — I didn't select her. Don't be so conceited!

[LEBANON *continues to explain.* MUNKITTRICK *is indignant;* DRUMDURRIS *endeavours to soothe him.* BROOKE *enters carrying a satin shoe, which he presents to* MISS MUNKITTRICK]

Brooke Twombley	Awfully sorry — what?

[BROOKE *hurries out*]

Miss Munkittrick	Where is Papa?

[IMOGEN *enters, carrying an aigrette*]

Imogen	Oh, Miss Munkittrick, what a shocking mishap!

[*They fasten the aigrette in* MISS MUNKITTRICK'*s hair*]

Miss Munkittrick	Have you seen my papa?

[LADY EUPHEMIA, *carrying a sash, hurries in as* IMOGEN *goes off.* MISS MUNKITTRICK *rises;* LADY EUPHEMIA *and* EGIDIA *adjust the sash hastily*]

Lady Euphemia Vibart [*Adjusting the sash*] My dear Flora, this is <u>too</u> unfortunate!

[BROOKE *re-enters with another shoe*]

Brooke Twombley	The other — what? [*To* LADY EUPHEMIA] There are some more pieces — come and help.

[BROOKE *and* LADY EUPHEMIA *hurry out*]

Miss Munkittrick	I want my papa! [*Seeing* MUNKITTRICK] Ah!
The Munkittrick	[*Giving her his arm*] Flora, we'll go home.
Miss Munkittrick	Pa, I'm not nearly <u>all</u>.

[*Her aigrette is very much on one side, her sash is trailing, and she limps away carrying one slipper*]

Egidia	Pray don't think of going!
Mr Joseph Lebanon	Let it blow over!
Earl of Drumdurris	My dear sir!
Mr Joseph Lebanon	Oh, very well, you're losing the best of the ball.

[THE MUNKITTRICK *and* MISS MUNKITTRICK *go out, followed by* EGIDIA *and* DRUMDURRIS. IMOGEN, LADY EUPHEMIA, *and* BROOKE *enter hastily, each carrying a fragment of* MISS MUNKITTRICK'*s dress*]

[*Taking the remnants*] Allow me — allow me — my affair.

[IMOGEN, LADY EUPHEMIA, *and* BROOKE *go out.* LEBANON *crams pieces of* MISS MUNKITTRICK'*s dress under a chair cushion*]

Let it blow over. Where's my partner?

[*He goes out.* MACPHAIL *enters with* MRS GAYLUSTRE *upon his arm*]

Mrs Gaylustre	Staying out is infinitely preferable to dancing, is it not, dear Sir Colin?
Macphail	Aye. I hate dancing.
Mrs Gaylustre	But your dear mother says you resemble some beautiful wild thing when you dance the Strathspey.
Macphail	That's because I hate it; the Strathspey's enough to make a lad wild.
Mrs Gaylustre	Witty boy!
Macphail	Eh, do you think I'm naturally quick?
Mrs Gaylustre	Quick?
Macphail	Quick in my understanding?
Mrs Gaylustre	I'm sure of it.
Macphail	Eh, I'm glad you think I'm quick.
Mrs Gaylustre	Why?
Macphail	Because Ballocheevin — that's our place, you understand — Ballocheevin is enough to soften a lad's brain.
Mrs Gaylustre	Then why hide your light at Ballocheevin?
Macphail	Well, the Macphails have lived there since eleven hundred and two.
Mrs Gaylustre	How romantic!
Macphail	So mother's just got out of the way of moving.
Mrs Gaylustre	Charming attachment to an old home.
Macphail	Aye, it's old. It hasn't been papered and done up since Robert Bruce stayed with us.
Mrs Gaylustre	Robert Bruce!
Macphail	Aye — just from a Saturday till Monday, I'm thinking.
Mrs Gaylustre	There must be a legend attached to every stone at Ballocheevin.
Macphail	Aye, it's interesting — but it requires papering. I am so tired of Ballocheevin.
Mrs Gaylustre	But you love the rugged country, the vast overwhelming hills and the placid lochs?
Macphail	Mother's been telling you that.

Mrs Gaylustre	Isn't it true?
Macphail	Eh, I am just weary of my native scenery.
Mrs Gaylustre	But what about the misty chasms of Ben-Muchty?
Macphail	That's an awfully damp place. That's where I caught my bad cold.
Mrs Gaylustre	And the gray shores of Loch-na-Doich? Your mother says you adore it.
Macphail	Eh, I am sick of Loch-na-Doich.
Mrs Gaylustre	And your feet don't ache to press the heather?
Macphail	It's when they're <u>on</u> the heather my feet ache. It's poor walking, heather.
Mrs Gaylustre	Then you don't watch the sun rise from the jagged summit of Ben-na-fechan?
Macphail	[*Cunningly*] Eh, but I do though, every day when I'm at home.
Mrs Gaylustre	But why?
Macphail	To get away from mother.
Mrs Gaylustre	Poor boy!
Macphail	[*Reflectively*] I've been thinking –
Mrs Gaylustre	Yes?
Macphail	That you'd better let go my arm now.
Mrs Gaylustre	Sir Colin!
Macphail	I've no personal objection, you understand; but mother's always looking for me.
Mrs Gaylustre	How thoughtless I am! [*He walks away*] Sir Colin!
Macphail	Aye?
Mrs Gaylustre	Your mother is driving you to contract this marriage with Miss Twombley.
Macphail	Well, mother's just making the arrangements.
Mrs Gaylustre	Your great heart hasn't gone out to her! Unhappiness must ensue! Your bright career will be dimmed!
Macphail	Will be <u>what</u>?

Mrs Gaylustre	Dimmed. What did you think I said? Oh, Sir Colin, don't carry this unsuitable bride to Ballocheevin!
Macphail	Well, it's a serious step; but I've been thinking it would be another in the house.
Mrs Gaylustre	You don't want another in the house. You need a strong, self-reliant wife who will take you out of the house.
Macphail	Eh?
Mrs Gaylustre	A woman, loving but firm, tender but enterprising, who will bear you from your dilapidated home and plunge you into the vortex of some great city. [*Suddenly*] Have you ever been to Paris?
Macphail	No.
Mrs Gaylustre	I know every inch of it!
Macphail	Madam!
Mrs Gaylustre	Oh, what have I said! Sir Colin, you have guessed my secret!
	[MACPHAIL *produces his ball-programme from his stocking and refers to it*]
Macphail	I'm engaged to Miss Kilbouie for this waltz, if you'll excuse me.
Mrs Gaylustre	[*Holding out her hand to him*] Colin.
Macphail	I'm thinking mother will be wondering –
Mrs Gaylustre	[*To herself*] Drat your moth – [*To* MACPHAIL] Never mind dear Lady Macphail for a moment. Colin, since you have discovered my love for you I will make no further reservation –
Macphail	But mother –
Mrs Gaylustre	[*Under her breath*] Drat your – [*To* MACPHAIL] Colin, I will be to you the wife you have described.
Macphail	I'm extremely obliged to ye – but –
Mrs Gaylustre	Hush, bold boy! [*She gives him a card*] You know my cruel brother takes me back to town tomorrow. Here is my address so that you may write to me constantly, devotedly.
Macphail	[*Reading the card*] "Mauricette & Cie., Court Dressmakers."

Mrs Gaylustre	[*Snatching the card from him*] That's a wrong 'un – I mean, that's a mistake. [*Giving another*] There. Hide it away, dear one – nearest your heart.
	[*He slips it into his stocking*]
Macphail	Oh!
Mrs Gaylustre	And now, as I start in the morning at nine-forty-five, sharp, on the tick, we must say farewell. Oh, this parting is too cruel. Colin!
	[*She falls against him*]
Macphail	Here's my mother!
	[*He throws her off*]
Mrs Gaylustre	[*Under her breath*] Drat your mother!
	[LADY MACPHAIL *enters*]
Lady Macphail	Madam. [*To* MACPHAIL] Why do you leave the ball-room, my lad?
Macphail	I've been just watching the moonlight on Loch Auchentoshan.
Lady Macphail	I am proud to see this devotion to Loch Auchentoshan, but tonight you have other duties almost equally important. After this paltry waltz we lose ourselves in the wild pleasures of our native dance.
Macphail	The Strathspey? [*He takes* MRS GAYLUSTRE'*s card from his stocking*] Oh! [*Hides it and produces his ball-programme from his other stocking*] The Strathspey.
Lady Macphail	Come, lad. They have yet to see the Macphail lead the Strathspey with his betrothed.
	[*They go out together*]
Mrs Gaylustre	Yes, and they shall ultimately see the Macphail writing love-letters to Fanny – love-letters with a promise of marriage in 'em. I'll consult a solicitor directly I reach town and be ready to marry or to sue him. Oh, Fanny, Fanny, ungrateful girl, what a lot you have to be thankful for!
	[*She runs out and* ANGÈLE *peeps in*]
Angèle	Milord! Miladi! [*She enters*] I must find miladi! Miladi!
	[LADY TWOMBLEY *enters*]

Lady Twombley	No news from Reeves & Shuckleback, the stockbrokers. The waiting for it will finish me.
Angèle	Oh, Miladi Twombley.
Lady Twombley	[*Turning to her sharply*] Ah!
Angèle	Tell me, vere is milord?
Lady Twombley	What! Has a messenger come from Strachlachan with a telegram for Lord Drumdurris? Speak?
Angèle	I do not know.
Lady Twombley	Oh!
Angèle	But, oh, miladi, I 'ave been a vicked girl!
Lady Twombley	I dare say you have – that's your business.
Angèle	Miladi, ze leetle Lord Aberbrothock is indispose.
Lady Twombley	The baby?
Angèle	Yees. To please milord, and contrary to miladi's ordares, I put Lord Aberbrothock to bed wiz his gun.
Lady Twombley	I know – I'm a mother – the child has swallowed the paint!
Angèle	Ah, yees!
Lady Twombley	Send a groom to Strachlachan for Dr. M'Gubbie.
Angèle	Yees, miladi.
Lady Twombley	Angèle!
Angèle	Miladi?
Lady Twombley	Tell the man to inquire at Strachlachan for telegrams for the Castle.
Angèle	Yees, miladi.
	[ANGÈLE *runs out*]
Lady Twombley	Oh, for a telegram from Reeves & Shuckleback! My diamonds, my double row of pearls for a telegram from Reeves & Shuckleback!
	[EGIDIA *enters with* ANGÈLE, *followed by* DRUMDURRIS]
Egidia	Lady Twombley!
Lady Twombley	Has Keith had a telegram?

Egidia	A telegram – no. My son is ill!
Lady Twombley	Oh, I know – he has nibbled his gun.
Egidia	His gun!
Angèle	Yees, miladi.
Egidia	Ah! The Army! [*To* DRUMDURRIS] So you have gained your own ends after all, Keith, and my boy has fallen.

[EGIDIA *goes out, followed by* ANGÈLE. DRUMDURRIS *sinks into a chair*]

Lady Twombley	Keith.
Earl of Drumdurris	Don't speak to me please, aunt.
Lady Twombley	I must. Reeves & Shuckleback are strangely silent.
Earl of Drumdurris	Let them remain so – I care not.
Lady Twombley	You don't care! Surely you are anxious to know whether you have been instrumental in saving me from – from growing my own vegetables?
Earl of Drumdurris	Growing your own –
Lady Twombley	Surely you want to know whether you have made me a wealthy woman or have ruined yourself in the effort?
Earl of Drumdurris	Ruined myself!
Lady Twombley	Keith, dear, I am afraid I haven't done what is strictly regular, but when you put me into communication with your stockbrokers I carried on my delicate little financial operations with them in your name.
Earl of Drumdurris	Aunt Kate!
Lady Twombley	Keith, you're annoyed!
Earl of Drumdurris	May I ask what delicate little financial operations?
Lady Twombley	I've speculated on the strength of my private knowledge of the decision of the Government on the Rajputana Canal Question – I mean <u>you</u> have speculated.
Earl of Drumdurris	Aunt Twombley, how dare you do such a thing?
Lady Twombley	How dare I! Boy – for you are little more – boy, you wouldn't have a Cabinet Minister's wife take advantage of her confidential acquaintance with her husband's official affairs to advance her own interests! Oh, Keith!

Earl of Drumdurris	But you've done it!
Lady Twombley	No, I haven't. Don't be so dull, <u>you've</u> done it.
Earl of Drumdurris	And if your delicate little financial operations –
Lady Twombley	If they come off, you have made what you men call a pile, Keith. All through your blundering aunty you will have made a pile.
Earl of Drumdurris	Which I hand over to you, Aunt Kate?
Lady Twombley	I shall borrow it, Keith, dear – may I?
Earl of Drumdurris	And if – pardon the question – if your delicate little financial operations –
Lady Twombley	Don't come off?
Earl of Drumdurris	Certainly; if they don't come off, what then?
Lady Twombley	Then through your reckless speculation you will have impoverished your estate for the rest of your life!
Earl of Drumdurris	Aunt!
	[EGIDIA *enters*]
Egidia	Keith!
Earl of Drumdurris	Tell me.
Egidia	Fergus has taken a turn for the better.
Earl of Drumdurris	Egidia, how can I look you in the face?
Egidia	Cannot we read a lesson from this dreadful occurence?
Earl of Drumdurris	To reconcile our views?
Egidia	Finally. You see how unfitted our son is to a soldier's life.
Earl of Drumdurris	Yes, I have been wrong. Happily it is not too late to remould his character. We must return to the ball-room.
Egidia	First come with me and peep into the nursery.
Earl of Drumdurris	By all means – the nursery.
Together	The nursery.
	[*They go out as the* DOWAGER *enters*]
Dowager	Katherine!
Lady Twombley	Dora?
Dowager	I am beside myself! Have you heard the news?

Lady Twombley	News? Telegrams for Keith?
Dowager	I know nothing about telegrams. I've just overheard Julian talking solemnly to Brooke. Do you know what your husband intends to do?
Lady Twombley	Grow his own vegetables.
Dowager	Bother his vegetables! He resigns his place in the Ministry.
Lady Twombley	The same thing. [*To herself*] Ah, why can't he wait!
	[SIR JULIAN *enters with* BROOKE]
Sir Julian Twombley	Katherine, I have been telling Brooke of the change in his prospects.
Brooke Twombley	I say, Mater, such a blow – what!
Lady Twombley	Pa, why can't you wait?
Sir Julian Twombley	Wait – for what, Katherine?
Dowager	Wait till the boy can patch up his future with a wealthy wife, of course.
Sir Julian Twombley	Really, Dora, I don't think it would be absolutely fair –
Dowager	Fair! People's actions are like their heads of hair – they can be dyed flaxen. [*To* BROOKE] Boy, why do you let the grass grow under pumps in this way?
Brooke Twombley	I haven't let the grass grow, Aunt Dora. I – ah – I have the happiness to be engaged – what!
Lady Twombley	Engaged!
Sir Julian Twombley	Bless my soul!
Dowager	In mercy's name, to whom?
Brooke Twombley	To Effie.
Lady Twombley and Sir Julian Twombley	
	Euphemia!
Dowager	Euphemia! Why, how dare you conspire to entrap a child of mine into a moneyless marriage?
Sir Julian Twombley	My dear Dora, you yourself suggested –
Dowager	If I may be guilty of such an expression – fall-lall!
Brooke Twombley	But, aunt –

Dowager	Hold your tongue, sir! Ah, I believe you all have abominable motives!
Lady Twombley	[*To herself*] The telegram! The telegram! Why is there no telegram!

[*The music of the Strathspey is heard.* IMOGEN *enters with* LADY EUPHEMIA]

Dowager	Euphemia!

[LADY EUPHEMIA *joins the others.* IMOGEN *goes to* LADY TWOMBLEY *in agitation*]

Imogen	Mamma! The Strathspey!
Lady Twombley	What of it?
Imogen	I'm engaged to dance it with Sir Colin. Oh, mamma, I don't love him!
Lady Twombley	Child, you loved him the other night while your head was being washed.
Imogen	I didn't see clearly then – the egg-julep was in my eyes. But now Lady Macphail is running after me, from one room to another, because she declares I must fulfil the destiny of a Macphail's betrothed and lead the Strathspey by his side. But I won't dance a deception before a room full of people!
Lady Twombley	Imogen, there is nothing for you but this marriage or contemptible, cleanly poverty.
Imogen	Poverty!
Lady Twombley	Child, you are young to be told these things – but what do you think is likely to happen to pa and me?
Imogen	Mamma, keep nothing from me.
Lady Twombley	In all probability we shall grow our own vegetables.
Imogen	Oh! What for?
Lady Twombley	For dinner. And, oh, Imogen, have pity on your mother! I can face contemptible, cleanly poverty with pa alone, but if I see my innocent chicks sharing our miseries every cabbage in our garden will grow up with a broken heart!

[*She embraces* IMOGEN. LADY MACPHAIL *enters with* MACPHAIL]

Lady Macphail	Miss Twombley, Lord Drumdurris's guests are politely waiting till you are pleased to lead the Strathspey with the Macphail.
Macphail	Miss Twombley.
Imogen	[*Quietly to* LADY TWOMBLEY] Mamma!
Lady Twombley	[*To herself*] No telegram from town. [*To* IMOGEN] Imogen, you had better not lose your dance.

[*With a slight courtesy to* MACPHAIL, IMOGEN *gives him her arm as* VALENTINE *enters, trimmed, shaven, and in immaculate evening dress*]

Brooke Twombley	Why, Val!
Lady Euphemia Vibart	Mr White!
Valentine White	Imogen!
Imogen	[*Leaving* MACPHAIL] Valentine!
Lady Twombley	Valentine White!
Valentine White	Imogen, am I too late?
Imogen	Too late?
Valentine White	For the honour of dancing with you tonight?
Imogen	You – you are in time, Valentine.
Valentine White	For which dance?
Imogen	This dance.
Macphail	Mother!
Dowager	The child's mad!
Lady Macphail	Stop the Strathspey! Stop the Strathspey!

[*She hurries out, followed by* MACPHAIL]

Sir Julian Twombley	Mr White, really you shouldn't, you know.

[*The music ceases*]

Valentine White	Sir Julian, Lady Twombley, with your permission I shall go no further to avoid the shams of life. I have found one cool resting-place in this world where there is reality and sincerity. [*With* IMOGEN's *hand in his*] And I have found in it an advanced state of civilization.

[*The* DOWAGER *pulls* IMOGEN *away*]

Sir Julian Twombley	I positively must beg –
Dowager	[*To* IMOGEN] Child, at this moment I feel grateful that I am your aunt, with all an aunt's privileges.
	[*She shakes her*]
Imogen	Mamma!
Lady Twombley	[*Seizing* IMOGEN] My chick, your mother has privileges also. Bless you and Valentine. [*Kissing her*] There! Dora, if you shake my girl again I – I'll slap you!
Dowager	Ah! Julian!
	[DRUMDURRIS *appears with a telegram*]
Earl of Drumdurris	Aunt!
Lady Twombley	What's that?
Earl of Drumdurris	From Reeves & Shuckleback!
	[*She snatches the telegram from him*]
Everybody	What's the matter?
Lady Twombley	Julian, look at your wife! Brooke, Imogen, come to your mother! No more worries by day and bad dreams at night! No poverty – no cottage – no – no – vegetables! I – I am a rich woman!
	[*She falls back fainting into* SIR JULIAN's *arms as they all surround her. At the same moment* LEBANON *rushes in with* MRS GAYLUSTRE. *He has a telegram in his hand; his aspect is wild, his face white*]
Mr Joseph Lebanon	Lady Twombley! Where is she? Lady Twombley!
	[*As* LADY TWOMBLEY *is assisted to a chair* LEBANON *falls into another*]
Imogen	Mamma!
Mrs Gaylustre	Joseph!
Imogen	Ah!
Mrs Gaylustre	Ah!
Sir Julian Twombley	Be quiet! Lady Twombley is ill!
Mrs Gaylustre	Ill! Look at Joseph! My only brother!
Sir Julian Twombley	Keith, explain this telegram or my brain will give way.

Dowager	No, no – tell me. My brain is stronger than Sir Julian's.
Earl of Drumdurris	[*To* SIR JULIAN *and the* DOWAGER *apart*] Mother – Sir Julian –
Mr Joseph Lebanon	I want a word or two with my friend, Lady T.

[MRS GAYLUSTRE *arranges his chair so that he faces* LADY TWOMBLEY. *She and* LEBANON *stare at each other*]

Mr Joseph Lebanon	Oh!
Lady Twombley	Ah!
Mr Joseph Lebanon	Lady T.
Lady Twombley	Hullo?
Mr Joseph Lebanon	I've 'ad a wire.
Lady Twombley	So have I.
Mr Joseph Lebanon	From Moss & Emanuel, my brokers.
Lady Twombley	Mine is from Reeves & Shuckleback.
Mr Joseph Lebanon	Oh, I see – <u>your</u> brokers. You've done me, Lady T.
Lady Twombley	Don't mention it.
Mr Joseph Lebanon	You're a knowing one.
Lady Twombley	I'm sure I'm very gratified to hear you say so.
Mr Joseph Lebanon	The Bills! Give me the Bills you swindled me out of!

[*He advances violently, but* MRS GAYLUSTRE *holds him back.* LADY TWOMBLEY *hands the bills to* SIR JULIAN]

Mrs Gaylustre	Jo!
Sir Julian Twombley	[*Giving them*] Mr Lebanon, the Bills, sir.

[LEBANON *snaps his fingers demonstratively in* SIR JULIAN*'s face*]

Mr Joseph Lebanon	Drum, thank you for your *recherché* hospitality. Carriage to the station in the morning, if you please. [*Kissing his hands*] Ladies – [*Breaking down*] Oh, Fanny, take me to bed!

[*He goes out.* MRS GAYLUSTRE *is about to follow when* LADY MACPHAIL *enters with* MACPHAIL]

Lady Macphail	Madam! My boy – my poor lad – has told me of your behaviour!
Mrs Gaylustre	My behaviour! He loves me!

Lady Macphail	Colin!
Macphail	I thought I'd just better mention the affair to mother.
Mrs Gaylustre	Of course; conceal nothing from your parent.
Macphail	And mother agrees with me –
Mrs Gaylustre	Yes?
Macphail	That it would be just a risky matter to correspond with a widow lady.
Mrs Gaylustre	Oh!
Macphail	[*Producing* MRS GAYLUSTRE's *card from his stocking*] So I'm thinking I shan't require this address.
Mrs Gaylustre	Ah!
	[*She slaps his face violently and runs out*]
Everybody	Oh!
Macphail	Mother!
	[LADY MACPHAIL *embraces him. The music of the Strathspey is heard again*]
	[EGIDIA *enters*]
Egidia	The Strathspey. Come into the ball-room. What has happened?
Lady Twombley	I can't enter the ball-room again tonight!
Earl of Drumdurris	But you must dance the Strathspey.
Lady Twombley	Must I? Dance then! [*They take their places for the dance*] Pa! Valentine, Imogen! Brooke, Effie! Keith, Egidia! Lady Macphail, Sir Colin! Dance! Dance with foolish, thoughtless, weak-headed Kitty Twombley for the last time, for tomorrow she becomes a sober, wise, happy, and contented woman! Dance!
	[*They dance the Strathspey and Reel –* SIR JULIAN *with* LADY TWOMBLEY, DRUMDURRIS *with* EGIDIA, BROOKE *with* LADY EUPHEMIA, VALENTINE *with* IMOGEN, LADY MACPHAIL *with* MACPHAIL. *The* DOWAGER *sits apart gloomily*]
Sir Julian Twombley	[*To* LADY TWOMBLEY *while dancing*] You've been indiscreet again, Kitty.
Lady Twombley	Finally, Julian, finally!

Sir Julian Twombley	No more extravagance?
Lady Twombley	Never! Never!
Sir Julian Twombley	And you resign yourself to a peaceful, rural life?
Lady Twombley	Oh!
Sir Julian Twombley	Promise me – promise me!
Lady Twombley	Ha, ha! Dance, pa, dance!

The End